How to Analyze People

Become A Master In Reading Anyone Instantly

+

Cognitive Behavioral Therapy

Master Your Brain, Depression And Anxiety

+

Emotional Intelligence

Master The Strategies To Improve Your Emotional
Intelligence, Build Self-Confidence, And Find Long
Lasting Success

+

Empath

How To Protect Yourself From Negativity
And Thrive As An Empath

-

A Four Book Bundle

Written By

George Muntau

Table of Contents

How to Analyze People

Cognitive Behavioral Therapy

Emotional Intelligence

Empath

How to Analyze People

Become A Master In Reading Anyone Instantly

Written by

George Muntau

Introduction

If there's a single most important skill you can pick up in today's globally connected and technically savvy world, it's the ability to analyze people. How do you determine a good fit for your organization while interviewing potential hires? How do you approach strangers? How about a crush or potential date? How do you build a stunning rapport with clients by diving into their head?

Learning to read other people gives you a definite edge in terms of predicting behavior, modeling your actions to build a favorable rapport with people, forging more fulfilling personal relationships and excelling at building professional relationships. No, I am not suggesting you switch careers to be an FBI agent. However, it doesn't hurt to possess their sharp people analyzing acumen, does it?

Some people unwittingly emanate signals that make them stand out as soft targets; others give out way too many aggressive signals for their own good. Being aware of your verbal and non-verbal communication patterns keep in greater control of conveying the intended things to people, and avoid any potential misunderstandings or conflicts.

The ability to analyze people impacts your relationship with them. When you develop a greater understanding of how someone feels or tailor your message/ communication pattern to make sure it is received as intended. Learning about reading and analyzing people helps you understand what clues you should be watching out for a while communicating with people. What are the things you should be carefully listening to? What are the typical signs that indicate how someone thinks or feels? How can you spot when someone is lying? How can you sense deception and dishonesty?

Glossies and periodicals such as Cosmo, GQ, and Psychology Today have a huge number of pages devoted to pop quizzes and pop psychology features such as "Ten Ways to Tell If a Man is Really into You" or "Tell Tale Signs Your Kids Are Lying to You: Watch Out for Their Feet Position to Know the Truth." Pop psychology has partially ruined the analyzing people game, by converting it into a non-serious, entertaining pursuit, which would be good if it wasn't so inaccurate.

In a more practical sense, this isn't how it works. You can't tell if a man is into you or not based on the shape of his eyebrows when he looks at you. Similarly, lying children can't be called out by looking at the direction of their feet. This makes for spicy, fun reading no doubt, but its applications are skewed. These publications and several other viral content sites are responsible for people leaping to unfortunate and unwarranted conclusions.

There are far more effective ways to tell how a person is thinking or feeling than eyebrows, the direction of one's feet and the color of one's eye.

Reading people is a vast and fascinating subject that has had realms of research pages dedicated to it. I attempt to condense all the important research, practical, actionable tips, and psychological techniques to come up with a concise guide to analyzing people. Think of this as the best of the best tips that will help you wade your way through reading people's minds and analyzing them for theirs and your benefit. From our personal lives to professional circles, the art of analyzing people is all-pervasive.

You really don't have to be a top-line interrogator to understand what is happening in someone's mind. There are signals, and if you're perceptive and trained to read these signals, you'll do well. People are almost always giving away important clues related to their thoughts, feelings, attitude, and actions. You simply need to know what to watch out for.

When you know exactly how someone feels, it is easier to empathize with him/her. It always gives you the power to negotiate better, build a more favorable rapport with someone and present the image you want to. Wouldn't you like to analyze people with the astuteness of Sherlock Holmes? Research has pointed to the fact that reading things like a person's body language can help you predict the outcome of a negotiation accurately about 87% of all times. How's that for an edge when it comes to sealing deals?

Even if you didn't realize it, all creatures are wired to reach each other's body language. Has it ever happened that you've experienced people completely or feel like you know them even though you've met them for the first time? Ever experienced love at first sight? Or had a nasty gut feeling about someone that turned out to be unfortunately true?

Our internal instinct or gut feeling often resonates within us based on the clues and signals it picks up from other people. Sometimes, observing people in pain or discomfort triggers a sort of pain in our head, which helps us vicariously experience what the other person is experiencing. Learning to analyze people helps you come close to experiencing what they are experiencing; thereby helping you make better judgments and decisions.

At a more subtle and complex level, we are all designed to be social and empathetic. However, only a few of us possess the knack of reading people and connecting with them at a seamlessly automatic and subconscious level. Specific parts of our brain automatically echo what the other person does or feels. For instance, have you noticed how someone you barely know smiles at you, your smile muscles activate almost involuntarily? On the contrary, when someone frowns, your frown muscles get activated too.

The human brain is automatically wired to pick up subtle clues that even our conscious mind may fail to register. For instance, when a person around is extremely angry and hides his feelings, we experience an almost instinctive feeling of discomfort around the person. He may not even look angry on the surface, but internally the body is reacting in the form of increased blood pressure or higher heartbeat rate. This is somehow picked up by our subconscious mind, which induces a sort of gut feeling that something about the person isn't right.

If you view it from the evolutionary perspective, plenty of our cognitive behavior can be traced back to resolutions gained from guessing what the other person is feeling or thinking. This is how we sought to solve most of our problems in the early evolutionary stages. We anticipated and guessed the other person's behavior in the absence of language only through their body language and expressions, and based our own actions or reactions to it.

The sharpest trial attorneys have an inherent instinct for reading and analyzing people. They gather insights from everything from the nod of a judge to the way the juror glances at the accused to the manner in which the opposing counsel speaks. They also go out of their way to train their clients in the art of keeping their verbal and non-verbal communication consistent with the image they intend to portray.

Clients are trained to give an impression of trustworthiness and innocence and eliminate any cues that indicate they are lying, which means minimal fidgeting, no darting eyes across the courtroom and appearing interested in their case.

Learning to interpret people's verbal and non-verbal communication will help you view them in a less judgmental and more objective manner. For instance, when someone compliments you insincerely (alright, you aren't the one who falls prey to these tricks), it is easy to get swayed by the person's talk. However, when you learn to analyze people, you can tell the truth from deception and protect your interests.

In the forthcoming chapters, I'll be sharing some of the best and most effective secrets for analyzing people, which will transform your interpersonal relationships, business dealings and social life in general. Hop aboard then and get ready to read people like a pro.

Advantages of Being a People Reader

Why must you know how to read or analyze people you ask? Well, there are tons of answers.

For starters, it saves you a lot of time, effort, energy, and emotions by dealing only with trustworthy and credible people. Can you imagine the heartache of having to kiss a thousand frogs before you find your prince? You'll learn to watch out for signs of qualities you seek in a potential mate and avoid wasting time on people who don't show any sign of alignment with your own personality or the traits you seek in your partner.

When you learn to read people like a pro, it's easy to understand their personality, attitude, values, and mood, before they can speak a single word.

It is easy to tell when people are being honest or truthful and when they are deceptive. This skill itself is useful everywhere from interviewing job applicants to choosing a date to know if you've been cheated by your spouse. Your partner or spouse will never be able to get away with cheating again.

Selecting a compatible dating partner by looking for qualities, values, personality traits and an attitude similar to yours. Determine if a person is truly interested in you, and then use that information to captivate their interest or impress them.

Boosting professional relationships and your career in general. When you understand what drives, motivates, inspires and channelizes people, it is easier to connect with them to fulfill professional goals, derive greater job satisfaction and maximize productivity.

You'll be amazed at how fast you may be promoted or get a raise with this invaluable ability to tap into people's emotions and channelize it optimally.

Boost your sales figures and multiply revenue by spending them only with clients who display favorable signs of purchasing from you. Knowing how to analyze a person will help you determine early signs of interest while interacting with prospective customers.

It will also help you negotiate better deals by pre-determining if a person is likely to agree to a higher price, thus raising your chances of acing negotiations. It helps you connect with absolute strangers, and makes you sway them in the desired direction. If you know that a person is reacting favorably when you mention to a particular figure, you can quickly close the deal. Similarly, if they appear apprehensive, you can quickly restructure your figures to make more sense to them.

Learning to analyze people also helps you make a stellar first impression. It is easy to be popular, trusted and credible in the first meeting when you know how to give the appropriate verbal and nonverbal clues.

Communicating with people is much more effective when you can read beyond their words. It gives you the power to interpret what's left unsaid. There is less scope for misunderstanding, conflicts, and drama. The communication is clearer, more effective and easily understood as intended.

Tuning into other's people's feelings and emotions allow you to be more empathetic towards them and reach out to them in times of distress, thus enhancing your interpersonal relationships. There is a greater opportunity to take control of the situation and avoid potential problems by doing things which are more favorable in the given circumstances.

Knowing how to read someone can be excellent for acing a job interview. You will know how the other person is talking to you, and continue doing things they subtly validate or endorse. You will also quickly stop doing things that don't seem to impress them much. Bonus – you can impress the interviewer with your mind reading skills (no, don't try it!)

As an interviewer or employer, it will save you the hassle, time and money of hiring the wrong folks. You'll develop a trained eye for spotting honesty, integrity, and capability. You'll be able to tell when people are telling the truth and when they are resorting to deception simply to create a favorable impression. You'll also determine if they possess the traits needed for a particular role. Interviewers can easily pick the most capable, determined and honest of the lot by applying people reading techniques.

Learning to analyze people's body language can make you an exceptional speaker. You'll realize when a person is truly interested in what you are saying (and keep the speech flowing in the same direction) or when you need to slightly adjust it to make it more appealing to the audience or when they are thoroughly bored listening to you (in which case a more dramatic action is needed to wake them up from their slumber).

Analyzing or reading your audience helps you gain information that can be built upon for establishing a common ground between them and you to make your speech even more relatable and persuasive.

For instance, if you are presenting a network marketing opportunity to people and their body language reveals that they are all ambitious people who love to lead a good life but who are thoroughly dissatisfied with their current jobs,

It is easy to influence, persuade and inspire people when you know how to read their thoughts and feelings. It is also easier to establish your authority, credibility, and integrity as a leader when you know how to read people's reactions to your actions.

People will be in a position to elect the right leaders simply by observing their body language for clues related to deception, integrity, empathy, and power. By observing the person's verbal and non-verbal communication patterns, you'll be able to gauge if they'd indeed be the right leaders.

You can simply tell when they are bluffing simply to come to power, and when they are genuinely interested in the welfare of people or making things better for people.

Chapter One

The Ultimate Non-Verbal Clue Cheat Sheet

It is often said that people convey much more through what they leave unsaid than what they actually speak. It couldn't be any truer. It is easy to say what we don't really mean but because that is controlled by our conscious mind. However, it isn't easy to hide nonverbal clues about what we are thinking or feeling because that is more of an automated process which is governed by our subconscious mind.

Therefore, tuning into these clues help us to connect with a person's subconscious, which is more challenging for him/her to control and manipulate, unlike words.

When we communicate with people, we are constantly giving and receiving wordless signals. All our nonverbal clues, including our facial expressions, gestures, the tone and pitch of our voice, the speed of which we are talking, gestures, eye contact, proximity to the other person and much more, convey powerful messages, even if we aren't aware of it. Often, these messages do not come to a standstill when we stop talking. Even in our silence, they end up communicating a lot.

People have much less control over the nonverbal messages they convey than what they actually speak. Non-verbal communication is more of an instinctive, emotional and reflex reaction that is more trustworthy than mere words, which can be consciously manipulated at will.

If there is a clear mismatch between what a person says and how he says it, non-verbal communication is generally granted more weight, because it is hard to stage-manage.

According to research, people retain about 10 percent of information given orally and about 20 percent of information given visually. However, 80 percent of the information given in combination (oral and visual is retained), which means people who communicate both orally and visually have a higher chance of putting their point across more persuasively and effectively.

Body language and other nonverbal clues are just as important (or in fact more) when it comes to reading and analyzing people. People are capable of retaining what they see more effectively than what they hear, which means if you are looking to analyze a person, pay close attention to their body language and other non-verbal clues.

When nonverbal cues match a person's words, it's a sign of trust, confidence, clarity and a comfortable rapport. On the other hand, when the nonverbal and verbal cues don't sync, it creates an atmosphere of mistrust, frustration, confusion, and tension.

Why, even lack of clear nonverbal messages is a tell-tale indication that the person is carefully manipulating his body language in order to hide his real feelings and emotions, which speaks a lot for itself.

Here are some proven tips and powerful guidelines for acing the nonverbal clues games.

1. Look for Clusters of Clues

One of the biggest mistakes people make while analyzing body language is looking for standalone signs, without viewing a cluster of clues. It works wonderfully for slick poker player flicks but not in real life. One often has to view a group of signs or actions to come to a reasonable conclusion about a person's feeling or behavior. For instance, a person may be making eye-contact, and you've been trained to believe that making eye contact is a sign of confidence, which means you ignore all other signs such as sweating, constantly touching one's face, etc. that reveal nervousness.

Always look for a cluster of clues rather than a single non-verbal clue. It is easier to manipulate a single clue than a bunch of everything else pointing to a clear thought or behavior pattern.

Spotting one cue shouldn't make you jump to an instant conclusion. For instance, a person may be leaning in the opposite direction from you not because they aren't interested but simply because they are uncomfortable. If you depend heavily on nonverbal clues, ensure that you spot at least three to four signs pointing to a clear thought process or behavior.

Try and take cues from different non-verbal communication sources. For instance, you may want to collectively analyze someone's tone, facial expressions, posture, hand gestures, etc. to be sure your analysis is accurate. Working in clusters increases your chances of reading an individual's behavior accurately.

2. Establish a Clear Baseline

It is important to have a clear reference or baseline for someone's behavior to analyze them well in general. There will be instances, of course, where you will be meeting and analyzing people for the first time. However, by getting to know someone better personally gives you insights and even make you more powerful. It gives a more well-rounded and wholesome approach to the analysis process.

Let's consider an example. One of your close friends is a very fast-thinking, swift acting and fidgety person. He is high on energy, and forever bouncing ideas off people. Someone who doesn't know this friend too well or doesn't have a baseline for judging him will inaccurately interpret his fidgeting as a sign of nervousness.

If you were to spot him on the street as a complete stranger, you'd believe he was nervous as hell. However, since you now have a clear baseline to understand he's hyperactive and excited about everything, you won't wrongly interpret his fidgety ways as nervousness.

Pay close attention to people's behavior all the time to understand their baseline. How do they behave and react in various settings? How is their speech and communication pattern in general? Are they in the habit of looking people in the eye? Does their voice undergo a transformation when they're particularly nervous? How do they react when they are deeply interested in something? How do they communicate when they are preoccupied or disinterested in something? These are critical points when making an effort to read people. It eliminates all the potential fallacies you can make while analyzing people.

When you spot inconsistencies in their regular baseline behavior, it will be easier to tell something is amiss. It will help you keep an eye out for non-verbal communication patterns that are not in sync with their regular behavior.

3. Body Language Cues

Though, this is a huge subject by itself that has consumed reams of paper and ink, let's get straight to the most crucial points. An individual's body language can convey a lot about how they think or feel. For instance, leaning forward or towards your direction when you are talking communicates that the person is listening to you keenly, and is interested in what you're speaking.

Similarly, limbs placed at the sides are an indication of being relaxed and in a positive frame of mind. Maintaining continuous eye contact is, in general, a sign of confidence, honesty, and positivity.

Similarly, crossing limbs while communicating with a person depicts the person is not open to or interested in what you are talking. They are more shrouded in secrecy, and not transparent by nature. Tapping fingers on the table of feet on the ground can be read as a sign of high nervousness. Similarly, when a person looks away while talking, he/she is almost always resorting to some sort of deception or is simply not interested in talking to you.

Crossed arms or legs are like barriers that indicate that the person isn't really in agreement with your ideas or what you are saying. Even if their expressions are pleasant or they are smiling, these physical barrier signs can be revealing. They are psychologically blocked from what you're saying. What makes this or any non-verbal near accurate is that the process doesn't happen intentionally, it is more involuntary.

4. Touchy Tales

Observing how people touch you can give you plenty of insights about their behavior and how they feel about you in general. Though, touch is a tricky one since most people have their own idea about touches based on their personal bubble. However, like most body language cues, it can give you a good idea about what the other person is thinking or feeling.

A weak handshake, for instance, could indicate uncertainty, hostility or nervousness. Similarly, the proximity of a person to you while you are speaking is a good indication of their interest in what you are saying or their feelings for you. People often distance themselves from others while talking when they don't wish to be intimate, affectionate or vulnerable.

Research by the Income Center for Trade Shows reveals that if you shake hands with an individual, the chances of them remembering you double. People view you as being more friendly, warm and welcoming when you shake hands with them.

While as a general guideline this is true, also take into consideration a person's baseline behavior. He/she may not be very comfortable being in close physical proximity to people, irrespective of the circumstances. Therefore, in such instances, a person maintaining a distance from you doesn't speak as much to you as it does to them.

Famous Hollywood talent scout/agent Irving Paul Lazar is famously quoted as saying that, "I have no contract with my clients. Just a handshake is enough." It speaks volumes about things and you can judge a person from their handshake.

5. Tone Tell Anyone

The tone of an individual's voice can convey heaps about how they are feeling. Listen closely for any inconsistencies in the pitch or tone of a person's voice. Are they coming across as predominantly excited or angry? Are they trying to hide something?

The volume of one's voice is also a reasonable and dependable indicator of how a person is feeling. If a person is taking louder or softer than usual, something may be amiss. Closely observe if a person is using more fillers than concrete words and sentences. It may be a huge indicator that they are hiding something, are nervous or trying to simply buy time to fabricate stories.

Sometimes, people's tone conveys very strong emotions that they are trying to hide or not expressing straightaway. For instance, a person may say the sweetest thing to you, but the tone can be more sarcastic, caustic or grudging. These may be the passive aggressive folks, who feel the need to address people or situations in a less aggressive manner.

Since about 80 percent of our entire message is communicated nonverbally, note other's words to read or analyze them. The meanings of some words can transform entirely when announced differently, thus making voice tone and inflection an important criteria for analyzing a person's behavior.

For instance, something as simple as the way you end a sentence can communicate a lot about how you are feeling. When you end the sentence an elevated note, you're turning a statement to a question or approaching the statement with an element of suspicion or doubt. This makes a person appear less assured and authoritative than intended.

6. The Cultural Context

Though some body language cues like eye contact and smile are universal, many nonverbal clues have a clear cultural context or baseline. For example, the Italian culture involves overtly expressive gestures such as plenty of waving, loud talking, excited voices and shouting.

In Italian culture, excitement is more conspicuously expressed than say in the UK. The non-verbal communication pattern is much more upbeat and loud, which can make it hard for the Italians to interpret the behavior of someone coming from a predominantly British or American culture, where the excitement is more subtly expressed. Therefore, viewing things in a cultural backdrop is important, especially if you're involved in doing business or forging political relationships with other cultures.

Even seemingly similar gestures can have an entirely different meaning in another culture. For example, while the thumbs-up sign (yes the same gesture through which we seek approval and validation on social media) is a symbol of validation in English-speaking nations, it is considered inappropriate in some regions of the Middle East and Greece. Similarly, while making an "o" sign with your forefinger and thumb is signifies OK in English-speaking nations, it is considered a clear threat in Arabic nations.

Personal space is almost sacred in Western corporate culture, so respecting associates and clients when they put up some barrier (like a bag or purse) is important. The amount of executives and managers who lose out on business deals for not interpreting these clues isn't even funny.

In addition to the cultural context, consider the overall context of the situation or circumstances under which the behavior occurs. Some settings (like a job interview) require a more formal behavior, so, sitting in a particular posture or gesticulating in a particular manner should not be misinterpreted. It can simply be attributed to the demands of the situation.

For instance, your body language at a pub when you are out with coworkers on Friday evenings varies considerably from your body language when you're with them at work. Non-verbal signals will vary according to the situation, so try to ensure that when you're analyzing people, you're also taking the situation into consideration. This will prevent you from wrongly reading a person who is spending a relaxed Friday night with co-workers as laidback, non-serious and disinterested.

7. Spotting Deception

It is both easy and tough to spot deception in a person. Easy, if you look for the right cues and know how to probe. It is tough because signs of deception and nervousness often overlap. However, it's important to read people and know exactly when they aren't speaking the truth.

Typical cues of lying include – maintaining minimal eye contact and constricted pupils, fingers on the mouth while speaking, faster than normal eye movements, the person usually tries to turn away from the person they are physically addressing, increased breathing rate, face, and neck region complexion changes, increased perspiration, change in manner of speaking such as stammering, pitch elevation, and clearing throat more often than usual.

When you notice any or all of these signs, don't instantly jump to the conclusion that the person is lying. A majority of these cues can also be signs of nervousness or fear (can be true in situations such as a job interview). If you want to ascertain if a person is lying, simply probe further and ask more questions to give yourself more time to determine the truth based on both verbal and non-verbal clues.

Reading nonverbal cues will vary from person to person. It comes only when you practice people watching and reading body language on the train, airport, and television (by turning off the sound). Closely notice people's actions and reactions.

When you observe them, try to decipher what they're thinking or trying to say. When there is a group of people, try to decode who the influencer or leader of the group is and get a feel of what they are discussing among themselves.

Even when you don't get an opportunity to gauge whether you are right or wrong in your analysis, you'll still develop a sharp, trained observational eye, which will come handy while communicating with others.

While watching out for the above-mentioned clues related to deception, it is also important to keep the person's baseline personality in perspective, along with cultural context and their behavior in other settings. Avoid making sweeping conclusions.

Some people are naturally awkward and nervous by nature. They tend to exhibit pretty much of the behavior mentioned above at regular intervals. Therefore, it is important to determine how the person normally behaves. If their mannerisms, gestures and eye movements are always a bit awkward, that's their personality.

Closely observe their body language and eye movements when you know for sure or have already established that they are speaking the truth. Compare or contrast this with their mannerisms when you suspect that they are not telling the truth. When you observe continuous change while making certain statements, you'll quickly gauge whether they are recalling facts/information or simply cooking up stories.

8. Nonverbal Cues on a Date

Assume it is your first date with someone. Can you imagine how incredibly helpful body language can be in helping you gain insights about the person's behavior/personality, which can, in turn, determine if he/she is a good match for you? Obviously, it's not easy reading people on first dates. Everyone's trying to put their best foot forward. You're also trying to be as charismatic as possible, while also expressing your interest in listening to what the person is saying. Where is the scope for analysis here?

Pretty much like everything else in life, with a little practice and keen eye, you'll learn to spot the right signals effortlessly, without investing too much time.

It isn't rocket science or anything overly complicated. Just tune into simple things like how guarded they are with their body. Initially, everyone will appear guarded. They will most likely cross their legs or arms, and keep a fair physical distance from you. The palms will generally be held facing them. This is reasonable on a first date.

However, as an observer you'll have to determine if it slowly transforms into a more open, warm and welcoming outing during the course of the date as the comfort level between you and the other person increases considerably. By observing their body language, you'll quickly know if they are genuinely interested in what you are saying and that if they are naturally connecting with you by demonstrating a more open body language.

We have the tendency to mimic or mirror other people's behavior. So, if you want the other person to look and feel more relaxed and less tensed, take on a more relaxed posture yourself. They will most likely mirror your actions and match your behavior.

Leave your arms uncrossed, give an honest smile, avoid physically distancing of yourself from the date, and reveal your palms. These cues convey that you are warming up to the other person, which will also make him/her comfortable. Of course, the level of comfort will keep fluctuating during the course of the date, and it will be nerve-wracking to maintain a standard demeanor. If you observe that a particular topic is stimulating a particularly negative body language, stop in your tracks and change the subject quickly.

9. Eye Contact

Renowned among lovers all over the planet, Shakespeare wasn't off the mark when he famously quoted that "the eyes are windows to the soul." Indeed, one of the most powerful nonverbal communication tools is eye-contact between two people. Maintaining consistent eye contact between people reveals trust, openness, genuineness, and sincerity.

Little eye contact during negotiation can prevent you from building a good rapport with the other person. It conveys to the other party that you're not straightforward, are acting evasive, and worse – you aren't honest.

Similarly, analyzing the other person's body language can give you insights in their personality or behavior. Are they avoiding your gaze? Are they acting shiftier and fidgety? They may not be the best people to do business with in that case.

Again, you need to spot a cluster of clues and not isolated nonverbal clues. Also look for any inconsistencies in the person's verbal and non-verbal clues. For example, a person may be fidgeting because he is nervous or new at this. He may just be hired to negotiate on behalf of an organization, and this may be his first project. When you look for other clues, you'll realize that the person is simply nervous and not necessarily dishonest. It is also natural to shift gaze when a person is involved in deep thinking or information processing.

Too much eye contact can also signify aggression, power and a more threatening approach. The other person may be trying to intimidate you by maintaining continuous eye contact.

10. Proxemics

Proxemics refers to the subject of personal space maintained between two people when they interact or communicate face to face. How many times have you felt uncomfortable when someone tried to stand too close to you while talking? The person is obviously trying to gain acceptance or validation from you or trying to make it into your inner circle.

Get others to respect your personal space and respect theirs too. If a person tries to come too physically close to you during negotiations, he may be trying to intimidate you or subconsciously coerce you into accepting his proposal. If you want to test a person's comfort level before making any move, simply stand or sit at a minimum of four feet away from them, and observe them closely to guess their comfort level.

If they look more open and welcoming, you are being invited into their personal space. If their body language is more rigid and closed, give them more time before jumping into their personal space.

11. Mirroring

Mirroring is mimicking or imitating the other person's nonverbal communication patterns subtly. When interacting with people or meeting them for the first time, check if the individual is subconsciously mirroring or mimicking your actions or behavior.

For instance, if you are seated across a table from another person, and suddenly rest your elbow or palm on the table, do they follow suit? Observe closely for about 10-15 seconds to check if they are subconsciously mimicking your actions.

Similarly, when you lift a glass to take a sip of water or drink, does this person follow your actions? If yes, it's good news. If someone is constantly mirroring your body language, they are keen on establishing a warm rapport with you or seeking approval from you. Try adjusting your actions or gestures to observe if the other person follows suit. You'll know soon enough if they are keen on establishing a rapport with you.

Chapter Two

Using Verbal Communication to Analyze People

Verbal communication is everything that is conveyed through written and spoken language. On the face of it, it may seem easier to decipher than non-verbal communication, however people are also experts at faking what they say, so its interpretation becomes slightly tricky and more meaningful only when combined with non-verbal communication.

Sometimes relying only on nonverbal clues can be tricky, and you will need verbal clues to complement the nonverbal clues for gaining a better understanding of someone's exact motives, behavior or personality. Imagine if you saw a person imitating a bird's flapping movement without knowing the setting or context. How would you interpret it? The person could be playing some game, he could also be demonstrating the movement of birds to someone, he could be drying himself, or he may be living in an altered state of mind, where he thinks he's a bird.

There are innumerable interpretations of a person's behavior and movements, which is why you cannot solely rely on nonverbal clues or body language for a comprehensive interpretation of a person's behavior or personality. You also need to probe further and watch out for verbal clues that reveal more about their motives, behavior, and personality.

For instance, a person may not be feeling too positive or upbeat, but may simply say they're not too bad. In this scenario, it is important to watch out for both verbal and nonverbal clues. Their words and the manner in which those words are uttered may point to the fact that they are in fact not too good.

In the above example, if the person says "not too bad" it can be interpreted as they aren't too good either. Of course, the person's regular verbiage and culture will determine how they usually speak, but their selection of words can reveal a lot about how they are feeling.

Let us consider another example. You open a nice new specialty restaurant in the heart of the city and have a steady stream of diners pouring in to try out the new dishes. Since the venture is still in its initial stages, you're eager to obtain feedback from your new customers to work with areas that need improvement.

You head to a family who has just finished eating their food for their feedback. The woman promptly says, "The soup was good." How would you interpret this? It can mean the soup was exceptionally good. However, there are higher chances that it means that nothing else was noteworthy except the soup.

When you learn to watch out for verbal cues, you're training yourself to read between the lines. People will often not spell out everything. They'll expect you to read their thoughts and feelings based on subtle verbal clues. For instance, don't we all hold a small grudge against people who say, you're looking good today. And we're doing the internal eye roll emoji thinking don't I look good every day, why just today? Some positive souls will interpret it as this means I am looking exceptionally good today.

There are plenty of hidden clues in what people say, you just have to listen and watch keenly to comprehend the right meaning.

Talking Too Much

Talking too much can be both - a sign of authority or a sign of trying to evade the real issue. It becomes all the more conspicuous when the conversation is peppered with a lot of fillers (aaaa, umm, hmm), silences and repetitions.

People who are trying to hide something or deflecting from the real issue aren't generally very concise in their verbal communication pattern. They try to buy time by hammering the same point repetitively using different words and phrases.

Confident people in positions of authority or leadership seldom talk fast or in an incomprehensible, rambling manner. They spread out their words, their tone is more even, and speak in clear, audible and coherent manner.

Similarly, people who are more self-assured, honest and open will convey things in a more concise, crisp and unambiguous manner. They may not always use the right words (dependent on language abilities). However, they'll communicate in a more coherent and synchronized manner. Their sentences are less peppered with gap fillers and ambiguous words and phrases that are more open to interpretation.

Verbal Modeling

It is human nature to be drawn to people who are similar to us. We naturally take to people who share the same interests as us, come from a similar cultural background, possess the same attitude as us and even speak like us.

Therefore, people who are constantly trying to match your words and talking speed may be eagerly looking to be accepted by you or please you. Doesn't this happen during job interviews?

Sometimes the interviewer is talking too fast, and the interviewee in his attempt to please the interviewer picks up the same speed or ends up choosing the same words and phrases subconsciously. This is referred to as mirroring in psychological lingo. You are simply mirroring the other person's words, actions, and attitude to impress them or demonstrate that "you're just one of them."

Acknowledgement

A person who is keenly listening to you cares about you or is interested in listening to you will almost always throw in verbal acknowledgments in the form of "yes," "yeah," "I understand how you feel," "wow," "sure," "really" etc.

These verbal interjections and acknowledgments communicate that the person has heard you out and understood what you're trying to convey. People who are disinterested or don't care about what you're trying to convey will be less likely to come up with acknowledgment words and phrases during the process of the conversation.

Beware if the acknowledgments are too frequent or over the top (if this isn't the person's usual baseline personality), it can be more contrived or fake.

Para Verbal Clues

Since we've already discussed in the chapter, how there are can be abundant scope for misinterpretation while deciphering verbal clues, para verbal clues (similar to nonverbal clues) help in adding more authenticity to our analysis.

Para verbal clues comprise everything from tone to pause between phrases to the speed of one's speech to the volume in which a person speaks.

Fast paced speeches can reveal a more deceptive, disorganized and uncertain demeanor, which is highlighted by ambiguous words and phrases. An evenly tempered speed can be an indication of self-assuredness, assertiveness, and balance. This person knows exactly what he wants, and is confident and comfortable expressing himself.

Similarly, a high voice volume can indicate authority or leadership. The person is trying to convey that he is in charge of the situation or trying to persuade people to accept his point of view or demanding attention.

There are several other verbal cues you need to watch out for while reading people. For instance, some expressions or sounds are used to complement words to make the message even more effective. Sometimes the message is too intense to be conveyed only with the help of words, which means you need to watch out for sounds like screaming, laughing, sighing and moaning to interpret the message accurately.

Word Clues

Notice how people are almost always dropping clues through their words. For instance, imagine a person has just stated that he's won another award. When you pay close attention to the choice of words, you'll realize that the person is trying to convey that he's won an award or several awards prior to this. He wants to ensure that people know he has done well previously too, thus boosting his image.

This person may be the kind who is constantly seeking validation, appreciation, and adulation from others to boost his self-esteem. He is likelier to be exploited using flattery and ego boosting praises.

Incongruence in Verbal and Nonverbal Cues

People can say anything they want, and they often lie through their teeth because they get away with deception. However, when you spot incongruence in a person's words and body language or expressions, you know something is amiss. For instance, someone is mentioning that they are really fond of someone, and while saying it, they are almost involuntarily shaking their head.

Notice how people sometimes say something makes them extremely happy, yet while saying it their expression is painfully somber. This can be revealing. However, don't jump to any conclusion until you are able to gather more information.

Practice your skills by watching chat shows, or talks show by turning the volume down. Try to guess what these people are saying simply by observing their expressions, gestures, and posture. When you're done writing what you think they are saying, watch again. This time turn up the volume and check if their words were congruent to their expressions or body language.

Pay Attention to the Emphasis

You may not be a trained FBI agent, but there are still lots of sneaky tricks and clever strategies that can be used to read people accurately. One of the most important verbal communication cues is the word a person emphasizes on while speaking. This reveals a lot about what is important to him along with his choice of words.

For example, if your supervisor says, I've decided to go ahead with this idea and emphasizes on "decided," there's little anyone can do to change his mind. He's conveying he has already made up his mind, and that there's no further scope for communication. Words reflect our thoughts and feelings.

The words we use are loaded with meaning, which consciously or subconsciously ends up revealing plenty of underlying emotions. Similarly, the words a person uses can a lot, communicate a lot about his personality. It is an indication of a personality that's not impulsive, more thoughtful and analytical. Look out for words people use (especially action words) while talking to you. It will tell you more than what people think they are giving away.

If someone constantly emphasizes on the word "hard" in saying I worked "hard" to accomplish this or it is "hard-work," they are most likely goal-oriented folks who love a good challenge and do not like to be given things on a platter. It also suggests that the person is capable of delaying gratification or holding off pleasure until they achieve the results they are after.

If a job application is constantly using the term "hard work" (yes I know they all do and they lie too in which case you have to look for a combination of clues to spot inconsistency in their verbal and nonverbal clues), he may be a more goal oriented and diligent employee, who doesn't shy away from taking up challenges or big responsibilities. He may possess the required determination to finish the given or assigned tasks, and can be dependable.

However, you have to be careful in situations like interviews, where people are aware that their personality, body language, confidence, etc. is being assessed in a more controlled and closed environment. This gives them the ability to manipulate the actions and body language to create the intended impression. However, if you have a trained eye and some practice, you'll quickly detect any inconsistencies.

Chapter Three

15 Brilliant Tips and Tricks for Reading People

Now that you've gained some expertise about analyzing people' behavior, let's sweeten the deal and give you even more amazing tips and tricks to read people like books.

Here are 12 amazing strategies that will give you insights into what people are thinking and feeling to help you understand them better, and develop even stronger interpersonal relationships.

1. Even seemingly innocuous questions such as "How are you today?" may be an attempt to establish your baseline, thus setting the stage for further probing and inquiries. This technique is typically used by salesman and business associates. If you're trying to establish someone's baseline, gently probe them about how their day was or how they are doing today. It opens the gates for further discussion, probing and negotiation.

Ask more open ended questions if you want to set an initial baseline for interpreting people.

2. Former FBI agent Joe Navarro offered many effective tips on reading people in Psychology Today, one of which included avoid vague questions after establishing a baseline. A rambling individual is tough to interpret. Therefore, ask straightforward questions that have a direct answer, which makes it easier for the questioner to detect deception. Don't look or appear too intrusive. Simply throw a question and observe minus interruption.

3. Clues that convey discomfort, stress, and distress include a furrowing brow, clenching jaws, compression of lips and tightening of facial muscles. Similarly, if someone is shutting their eyes for longer than a regular blink or clearing their throat, there's a high chance they're stalling. Leaning away from you or rubbing hands against their thighs or head is also a sign of high stress.

4. Children are brilliant subjects to practice on when it comes to detecting liars. If you're looking for signs to spot a liar, simply observe what children do when they

lie. Annie Duke, a renowned professional poker player, and cognitive psychology doctoral student suggested that kids are an excellent source to pick up cues about deception.

Adults pick up deception skills to bolster social interactions and personal relationships, which kids haven't mastered at that stage. Therefore, they are pathetic at lying. Every sign is clearly visible because they aren't yet adept at the art of lying. Therefore, observing clear signs of deception in them gives you the ability to spot the same signs in adults.

This, of course, comes with its own fine print. Some people will be better at lying than others. Those who have mastered the art of deception will obviously be well versed in hiding signs of untruth.

5. When someone nods excessively in an exaggerated manner, it means he is simply conveying his anxiety about your opinion of him. The person is also likely to think that you aren't confident about their abilities.

6. Our brains are by default hardwired to interpret power or authority with the volume of space occupied by someone. For instance, an erect posture with

straightened shoulders conveys authority. It communicates that you are occupying the optimum available space.

On the other hand, slouching is occupying less space and presenting yourself in a more collapsing form, thus demonstrating reduced power. People who maintain a good posture automatically command respect on a subconscious level.

7. Genuine smiles are easy to tell apart from contrived or exaggerated smiles. When a person is genuinely delighted to see you or by the conversation they're having with you, their smile reaches the eye. It also slightly crinkles one's skin to form crow feet. Smile is the single largest arsenal people use to hide their true feelings and thoughts.

If you want to tell whether a person is smiling genuinely, watch out for crinkles near the eye corners or crow's feet on the skin. The smile is most likely a deception in the absence of these signs.

Did you know that a genuine smile is called a Duchenne smile? It is believed that a smile can never be faked, however hard a person tries. Have you ever wondered why you or someone ends up looking so awkward in pictures? It may appear on the face of it that we're smiling, but we're actually only pretending to smile. Since a genuine smile elevates your cheeks a bit, there are bound to be some crow's feet, which bundles up just below the eyes. Body language experts say this is tough to fake.

You actually need to experience a happy or joyful emotion to be able to create that expression. When you're not comfortable from within or not experiencing genuinely happy emotions, the expressions just do not fall into place.

8. Look out for micro expressions. If you observe people closely, you'll notice that their real thoughts or feelings (and not what they're trying to convey deceptively) will be flashed on their face in the form of micro expressions.

Sometimes, while trying to come across as consoling, they'll quickly let off a smirk that can last 1/15th of a second. This is because their thoughts and expressions are syncing involuntarily for a moment.

Next time you're traveling by aircraft, notice how flight attendants smile with the help of their mouth but their eyes are blank, and the eyebrows are in a positioned in a scowl when you ask for more drink.

The truth almost always slips out in the form of these tiny expressions or micro expressions. While it isn't difficult to fake body language, look out for the not so subliminal cues, which are a clear giveaway. It's pretty much like shooting stars; you've got to see it fast before it disappears.

9. Avoid making assumptions. One of the best tips you can receive while analyzing people is not to make prior assumptions or have any sort of biases or prejudices. Sometimes we get to analyze people with a clear prejudice and think we've already found what we've been seeking. For example, if you assume (based on prejudices etc.) that a person is angry, then all their actions and words will seem like there's a deeply hidden anger within them. You will find only what you are looking for.

For instance, if we go to a person's workplace assuming that he is totally disinterested in the job or dislikes it, we'll assume his concentration or lack of cheery approach as absolute disinterest in the job. He may be strictly trying to focus on his job as opposed to hating it. Not everyone grins and laughs when they are enjoying their work. Sometimes, they are just involved in performing it more diligently.

Another important point is to avoid judging others people's personalities based on your own. For instance, in the above scenario, if you truly love your job, you'd have a more positive, grinning and happy expression as opposed to a more somber look. However, not everyone shares your unique traits, behavior, attitude, beliefs, and values.

10. Identify behavior patterns. Take for instance you're flying in an aircraft, and a particular cabin crew member looks really pissed off while talking to a passenger seated near you. Now, you can quickly jump to the conclusion that he/she has an inherently arrogant, impatient and hostile personality.

However, he/she may have just fought with his/her partner before boarding the aircraft, and may still be carrying the anger within him/her. You really can't tell if it's the former or later until you observe a clear or repetitive pattern.

Does she look particularly annoyed when passengers ask for something? Well, then you've spotted a pattern. If not, you're just being plain unfair in judging him/her based on a single isolated pattern that originated due to another external situation (argument with her partner) Looking for patterns helps you analyze people more objectively and accurately.

11. Compare behavior. When you've noticed that someone is behaving particularly out of sync with a group of people or in a specific setting, observe whether they display the same behavior in other groups too. Also, if someone is acting slightly off the normal course with a person, try and gauge if they repeat the same actions with others too.

Continue to observe the person's actions in multiple settings to gain a comprehensive insight of his personality or behavior. Does the individual's expression or gestures change? Does his posture undergo a transformation? What about the voice and intonation? These clues help you know if the behavior you observed initially is a norm with them or simply an exception.

12. Notice people's walk. The way a person walks can reveal a lot about him. People who are constantly shuffling along demonstrate a clear lack of coherence of flow in things they take up.

Similarly, people walking with their head bowed reveals a lack of self-confidence or self-esteem. If you do observe one of your employees walking with their head down, you may want to help build the person's spirit. Appreciate him more in public and give him tasks that demonstrate your faith in him. Approach him by asking him open-ended questions during meetings to get him to talk more and bounce ideas off people.

13. Power play with voice. Much as people like to believe, the most powerful or commanding person is not the one at the helm of the table. It is the person with a confident, firm and strong voice. Confidence denotes power.

At any conference table or business lunch, the most powerful and influential/persuasive individual is the one who has a confident and commanding voice, and a huge smile (smiling is a sign of effortless confidence almost like the person is so good, he doesn't have to try too hard).

However, do not confuse a loud voice with a confident/strong voice. Merely speaking loudly won't earn you respect if you sound shaky and confused.

When you're pitching an idea/product to a group of decision makers or people in general, watch out for people with the strongest and firmest voice. These are the people the leader may generally rely on for making decisions or these are the group influencers. When you learn to observe and identify the strong voices, your chances of a positive outcome increase drastically.

People in power often keep their voice low, relaxed and maximum pitch. They don't speak in a tone that elevates in the end as if they are asking a question or sounding uncertain/doubtful about something or looking for approval. They will spell their opinion in a more statement like manner by employing a more authoritative tone that elevates in the middle of a sentence, only to drop down in the end.

14. Stand opposite a mirror to observe your own body language. Give yourself various scenarios (party, informal outing with friends, a business presentation) and start talking like you would in these settings.

Being aware and conscious of your own body language in varied settings will help you identify patterns of other's body language too. Not just the mirror, the next time you find yourself at a negation table or first date, try to be more aware of your body language and the impression you are trying to convey. This will help you decipher the other person's thoughts and emotions more effectively through their body language.

Observe your own body language without being self-conscious or judgmental. Look how your eyes light up when you are talking about someone you care for deeply, notice how your eyebrows crink when you are speaking to someone you don't really like or trust. This will help you gain a better understanding of other people's thoughts and feelings.

Notice everything from your eye movements to gestures to posture. This will help you to exactly understand what you need to watch out for while analyzing other people.

By tuning into your own underlying feelings and emotions, you will be able to judge other people's body language, words and actions more accurately.

15. When people try to manage their body language by misleading others, they concentrate on their postures, facial expressions, gestures, and postures. Since their legs movements are more unrehearsed, this is where you're most likely to find deception. When in stress and duress, they will display signs of nervousness, fear, and anxiety with their legs.

If you watch closely, their feet will fidget, shift and wrap around each other make increased movements. The feet will involuntarily stretch, kick and curl their feet to eliminate tension.

Research has revealed that people readers will enjoy higher success analyzing a person's emotional state just by observing his/her body. Even though you may not be aware of it until now, you've been intuitively responding to leg and foot gestures all the while.

Chapter Four

Decoding Personality Types

The study of personality is broad, varied and evolving. Different schools of psychological study have come up with different theories about analyzing personality, including dispositional (or trait based study), biological, social learning and psychodynamic.

Personality refers to a person's unique characteristics related to feeling, thinking, and behavior. It emphasizes predominantly on two areas – understanding differences between people with regards to specific characteristics and the bringing together all characteristics to understand the person as a whole.

Let's take a look at some psychological personality types to help us gain a better understanding of people's baseline, which can then be used in combination with verbal and non-verbal cues to help us read them even more accurately.

Type A, B, C and D Personalities

The Type A and Type B personality theory was first introduced by cardiologist duo Ray Rosenman and Meyer Friedman in the 50's.

Type A was known to be at a greater risk of coronary heart diseases than Type B since the former are known to be short tempered, highly competitive, sensitive, proactive, multitasking, impatient, and always in a hurry. Type A personality people demonstrate an ambitious, hard-working, status conscious and aggressive disposition. They are always anxious to accomplish, which in turn leads to higher stress.

Type B, on the other hand, is known to be reflective, even-tempered, innovative, less competitive, low on stress and unaffected by time constraints. If you're a classic Type B personality, you are moderately ambitious, live at the moment, and work more steadily. Type B folks are social, procrastinating, creative, easy-going, modest, mild-mannered, and lead a more stress-free, laid-back life.

Later theories (that evolved to encompass even more personality types) found it constricting to divide all people into a Type A or Type B personality. Some people displayed characteristics predominantly from Type A but also displayed Type B traits. Thus, it became obsolete to classify people into two personality groups, which is why more personality types evolved.

A typical Type C individual has a fastidious eye for detail and is focused. They are inherently curious and are constantly trying to figure out things. There is a strong tendency to put other's needs before yours, and avoid being assertive or speaking up. Typically, Type C will never mention straight away if they like or dislike something. Over a period of time, this leads to resentment, stress, and depression. They take everything in life seriously, which makes them dependable workers. Possessing great analytic skills, and intelligence, they just need to develop some assertiveness and learn to relax a bit.

Type D people have a more negative perspective of life and thrive in pessimism. Even a tiny event is enough to mess up their entire day. They tend to be more socially withdrawn and suffer from a deep seated fear of being rejected, even when they enjoy being with people. They are at a higher risk of suffering from mental ailments since these folks predominantly lean towards melancholy and pessimism.

There is a greater tendency to suppress emotions, making them more prone to anxiety and depression. They expect the worst in any situation and do not share the feelings or emotions with people easily owing to the fear of rejection.

Trait Theory

The trait theory is primarily concerned with establishing the fundamental traits that provide a meaningful or coherent description of an individual's personality. It is also concerned with measuring these traits.

How does one draw a conclusion about an individual's personality based on the trait theory? He attempts to answer questions related to his feelings, thoughts, actions, and attitude. With the help of a personality inventory and rating scale, the individual's personality is determined. It is a combination of his responses and observation by the assessor.

Trained psychologists who observe these individuals rate them on a bunch of questions such as, how would you rate the individual's self-confidence? How would you rate the given subject's emotional balance?

Individuals are rated on a number of traits such as integrity, perseverance, sociability, dominance, etc., which in turn offers an analysis of the individual's personality.

Psychoanalytical Theory

This theory is dramatically diverse from the trait theory. While trait theory mainly relies on analyzing people based on what they've stated about themselves, psychoanalytic theory is an in-depth analysis of unique individual personalities.

Since the motivation is essentially more unconscious or subconscious, the analysis is believed to be more accurate. In the psychoanalytical theory, an individual's verbalization and behavior are considered to be a disguised manifestation of his most underlying subconscious/unconscious mind emotions.

The theory was first put forth by Sigmund Freud, when he compared a person's mind to an iceberg, where the surface makes up for our conscious experience, while the bigger masses under water level represent our unconscious (comprising impulses, most primitive instincts and deep passions that influence our actions and thoughts.

Freud's much referenced psychoanalytic personality theory proposes that all human behavior is the direct result of interactions between id, ego, and superego. This specific structural theory of personality focuses on the role of our unconscious/subconscious mind in modeling our behavior, actions, and personality.

Through the method of free association (dreams, experiences, childhood memories), Freud discussed analyzing people's most underlying feelings and emotions that determine their present attitude, behavior, and words.

Thus most behavior patterns and actions are traced back to the individual's early childhood experiences or memories that they aren't consciously aware of; but are still lingering in their unconscious mind.

For instance, if a person displays more aggressive tendencies, it can be attributed to violent or aggressive experiences faced during their early childhood. If there is too much of a need to be accepted or please people, it can be traced back to being rejected by family members or friends.

Psychoanalysis is still widely used for helping people with issues such as depression, anxiety, panic attacks, obsessive behavior, aggression, anger issues and more.

Social Learning Theory

This theory proposes that people pick up personalities or behavior patterns based on their learning from the immediate environment, and as such variations in behavior are a direct result of the diverse conditions in which we learn while growing up. Certain behavior patterns or personality traits are picked up through direct experiences.

For instance, an individual behaving in a particular manner may have been rewarded for it earlier, and hence is simply repeating what he learned through his direct experiences. For instance, someone constantly throwing tantrums and big on drama may have learned through early direct experiences that doing this helps them receive plenty of attention, which then becomes a behavior pattern. However, responses can also gain without direct experiences.

Since the human mind utilizes complex, symbolic codes to retain information based on observations, but behavior can also be a result of observing other's actions and consequences. Much of our observations and experiences are vicarious and complex. Reinforcement may not be needed for picking up or imbibing certain personality traits.

Carl Jung's Classification

Noted psychologist Carl Jung classified an individual's behavior or personality, based on their sociability, as introverts and extroverts.

Introverts are people who are predominantly shy, withdrawn and reticent, talk less, and are not comfortable in social settings. They tend to be more fixated on their ideas and are known to be sensible. It isn't easy to get them out of their shell and develop a rapport with everyone.

Extroverts are gregarious, outgoing, talkative, generous, courageous and friendly. They are the classic "people's persons" who live more for the present than worry about their future. Their disposition is happier go lucky and positive. Challenges do not shake them easily.

Later, psychologists added another type to Carl Jung's classic classification theory. They argued that only a handful of people display extreme introvert or extrovert tendencies. A majority of folks, in fact, possess qualities of both an introvert and extrovert. These people are referred to as ambiverts.

Ernest Kretschmer's Classification

German Kretcschmer's classification theory attempted to connect an individual's physical characteristics with his personality, and certain mental ailments that they were most likely to suffer from.

He classified people into various types including Pyknic, Asthenic, Athletic, and Dysplastic. Pyknic types are folks who are short and round. They are said to display personality traits of an extrovert - known to be outgoing and gregarious.

The Asthenic types, on the hand, are people who have a slim/slender appearance. They possess a predominantly introvert personality. The Athletic folks are people who have strong, well-built and robust bodies, who display more aggressive, energetic and ambivert traits.

The Dysplastic type essentially displays a disproportionate body and is not a part of any of three previously mentioned types. The disproportion is due to a hormonal imbalance, where a person's personality also reveals traces of imbalance.

Psychological Analysis of Personality

Briggs Myers Type Indicator

There are several personality tests that individuals can take to have a psychological analysis of their most predominant personality. One of the most popular ones is the Myers-Briggs Type Indicator. It is a comprehensive and more reflective self-report that offers an analysis of people's personalities based on the manner in which they view the world, and wield decisions.

The test was created by Katharine Cook Briggs and Isabel Briggs Myers (Katharine's daughter). It relies on the Carl Jung's typological theory where he proposed that there are four essential psychological functions experienced by humans - thinking, intuition, sensation, and feeling.

In every person, Jung stated, one of the four fundamental functions dominates over others. The MBTI focuses on naturally found differences between different types of people, with a fundamental assumption that every one of us possess a clear preference in the manner through which we experience the world around us, and these differences, in turn, underline our needs, beliefs, values, interests, and motives.

According to this popular psychological personality test, there are about 16 varied types of personalities. The test consists of a bunch of questions, where the respondents' answers demonstrate their personality type. It also offers insights on how a particular personality is most suitable for success in different areas such as career, interpersonal relationships, etc.

Here are the 16 main personality types as defined by the Briggs-Myers Type Indicator.

1. INTJ

These folks are predominantly imaginative, creative and strategic. They seem to have a ready plan for almost everything in life.

2. INTP

Innovative, analytical, logical and curious, they rarely stop reasoning and questioning things. They are essentially inventive, intelligent and creative.

3. ENTJ

These are your natural leaders. They are courageous, imaginative, unafraid of taking risks, bold and extremely strong-willed. They rarely fail to find a way or in the absence of it, will create the way themselves.

4. ENTP

The quintessential debaters, who can never resist a challenge that stimulates their intelligence, these folks are smart, argumentative, quick-witted and curious.

5. INFJ

There are the unflinching idealists of the Briggs-Myers personality test. They are tireless, inspiring, calm and mystical. The kind who let their actions speak louder than words.

6. INFP

These are the compassionate, kind, considerate, poetic, altruistic people, who never step back from contributing to a worthy cause.

7. ENFJ

These are people magnets, the charismatic, persuasive and inspiring leaders who can hold their audience spellbound.

8. ENFP

They are creative, innovative, free-spirited, sociable and always cheerful. These folks enjoy forging strong social and emotional bonds with others, and are often the proverbial "life of a party."

9. ISTJ

Their reliability and dependability can seldom be questioned when it comes to offering practical solutions. Fact-minded, high on integrity and analytical, the ISTJ personality types are accurate, patient and responsible.

10. ISFJ

The ISFJ people are warm, devoted, protective and forever ready to put their loved ones out of harm's way. They are kind, altruistic, enthusiastic and generous. They possess well-evolved people and social skills.

11. ESTJ

They are known to be exceptionally good administrators with an unsurpassable ability to manage things, people and situations.

12. ESFJ

Their caring and empathy quotient is above average, which tends to make them extremely popular and social. They are always ready to step in when people need help and make for exceptional sounding boards or counselors.

13. ISTP

These are the quintessential risk-takers, who don't shy away from wielding courageous and bold decisions. They are forever experimenting and trying to master varied skills.

14. ISFP

Flexible, adaptable, magnetic, charming and artistic, they are always eager to explore new things and thrive of novel experiences.

15. ESTP

These are smart, enthusiastic and perceptive people who live a life on the edge. They are intelligent and make for energetic conversationalists.

16. ESFP

The ESFP personality type is enthusiastic, entertaining, spontaneous and energetic. Few other personality types are able to motivate and encourage others as much as these folks do. They have the most powerful aesthetic sense.

The Briggs Myers test is widely used in professional settings for leadership development, career selection, screening potential employees, promoting workforce and team building.

Of course, like most other theories, it has earned its share of criticism for not being conclusive enough or generating "soft" results that cannot be completely applied in a business setting. However, despite the criticism, the test still offers a reasonable reading of a person's personality and can be a good value addition when it comes to reading/analyzing people. It can be more conclusive when conducted in combination with other psychological analysis techniques.

Certain types of personalities are more suitable for specific situations than other types. Knowing where others or yourself fall on the rating scale makes it easier for you (as a decision maker) to know where people are most likely to be comfortable.

For instance, knowing that someone has a more introvert type personality will help you make the most of their preference of working in structured, tinier, quieter and more organized settings. You'll quickly figure out that these people may not thrive while working in a team, and are more likely to maximize productivity by working alone. Similarly, extroverts may flourish in huge, loud settings, surrounded by lots of people.

The Briggs Myers can offer a reasonably accurate (though not comprehensive) baseline for helping you analyze people using a bunch of other psychological and practical people reading techniques.

Chapter Five

Communication Styles
of Different Personalities

One of the best and biggest advantages of analyzing people is being able to communicate with them more effectively. It is about forging strong professional connections, building more fulfilling interpersonal relationships and minimizing the scope for conflict.

An individual's inherent communication style is determined by the manner in which he/she interacts with or attempts to interact with others. It is determined in the way they relate to other individuals and how what they say is generally interpreted.

Different personality types are known to communicate in different ways. For instance, in the Briggs Myers personality, ESTJ people may find it easier to communicate within the ST personality group (ESTJ, ESTP, ISTP, ISTJ) than say people from the NF (ENFJ, INFJ, ENFP, INFP) personality group.

Since the Briggs Myers is known to be one of the most comprehensive categorizations of people's personalities, it is valuable to know how each personality type communicates and how to communicate with them to achieve optimal and favorable results. These insights can be used anywhere from interpersonal relationships to professional settings to hobby clubs.

You can determine the personality types of your employees or new hires, or business associates, and use the approach that works best for them while dealing with them for maximizing productivity. The Briggs Myers personality test can be excellent for everything from hiring new employees to analyzing the personality of a potential life partner.

When you know the communication style and preferences of each personality type, it is easier to communicate with them in a more connected and relatable manner.

This is simply because ST people process information and communicate it in a more logical manner than NF people, who are more emotional and intuitive in their communication.

The ST Group

ESTJ

ESTJ people are more open, logical and demanding in their approach to communication. They are essentially deadline oriented and expect things to be completed as discussed and agreed. You won't get too far by involving topics that stimulate an emotional response. Rather appeal to their logical side by offering features/benefits, using more visual aids, offering examples and demonstrating immediate benefits. They often find it hard to express their inner most feelings.

Their people skills aren't much evolved especially when it comes to being patient and gentle with people. The communication style is more open, straightforward and direct, which can hurt other personality types or worse, provoke them.

Stick to practical solutions, data (to back you arguments) and exchange of logical opinions while communicating with the ESTJ type.

ESTP

ESTP type people are dynamic and active communicators and know how to influence, captivate and persuade others through words. Some people can be offended by their direct approach though. Bring variety while communicating with an ESTP personality type. Be more energetic and enthusiastic when you're trying to persuade them.

Like ESTJ, they aren't very comfortable talking about emotions and feelings and like to keep discussions focused on practical, actionable solutions. They address and approach issues with a more rational angle. Be solution-oriented if you want them to get things done or buy your idea. Winning their affection becomes fairly easy when you can put forth logical arguments and practical solutions.

ISTJ

ISTJ type people are natural, straightforward and open communicators. They lay emphasis on precision in their communication pattern. You won't cut it with them by presenting vague arguments and figures. These guys are sticklers for exactness and rules.

They are action oriented and practical in their strategies, which is why most other personalities make a beeline for them when wise, actionable counsel is needed. They find it tough to discuss or talk openly about issues related to love or other emotions. It just may not evoke the desired response from them. Stick to rational discussions, and convince them with precision and accuracy.

Since they are specific, self-assured and logical by nature, they appreciate specifics, confidence, and reasoning. Appeal to logical side by offering well-thought and researched analytic arguments. Demonstrate instant advantages and benefits, while selling ideas, arguments or products to them. Always offer them clear examples and utilize visual aids while explaining concepts.

ISTP

ISTPs are again more direct in their communication and similarly, appreciate a straightforward and open communication approach. They don't take too well to individuals who possess an overly demanding personality.

The ISTP personality type is not very comfortable when it comes to showing tact, empathy or consideration. Some people are invariably affected by their direct and open style of expressing opinions. Again, the ISTP too, struggles with emotional experiences. They find it tough to express their inner feelings.

Don't focus too much on feelings and emotions if you really want to make the communication easy and relatable for them. On a personal front, come up with more practical measures as well as actionable strategies to address their everyday problems.

Professionally, again, exchange more logical arguments or tangible solutions that appeal to their sense of reasoning.

The NT Group

ENTJ

ENTJ highly appreciate manners, order, decorum, and respect. They may appear more demanding when it comes to important issues. They love to swap or exchange views with others, with the fine print that they will go all out to ensure that their opinion alone is right.

Their approach while interacting with people is more business-like, self-assured and objective. It can come across as bossy, but that is the way they communicate. They like confident and business-like communicators who come straight to the point in a professional manner.

They aren't completely at ease when it comes to demonstrating virtues such as tact, patience or emotions. ENTJs are more intense in their professional communication. Ask for their authoritative or expert opinion on any matter if you really want to impress them. Discussion of ideas, practical solutions and analytical opinions related to various subjects may help you win their attention.

INTJ

INTJs are constantly engaged in the pursuit of trying to find out how things are structured, and what changes can be brought about in the structure for good. Their communication pattern and personality essentially involves figuring out the minutest details about things, and them improving it.

They are pleasant and easy conversationalists, without an air of arrogance or formality, but they don't appreciate over familiarity too quickly. Take time in establishing a rapport with them rather than trying to act overtly friendly on the first meeting itself.

The INTJs, pretty much like others in the NT group, struggle with diplomacy and patience in dealing with people. They stick to tradition and established norms even though they may believe it to be a mere formality.

Don't resort too much to emotional topics while interacting with these guys. If they are deducing a concept or argument, make some critical or intelligent comments about the concept to win their admiration.

They appreciate communicating with people who make to the point and well-thought arguments. INTJs are introverts by nature, but they are capable of spreading the enthusiasm and energy when that took in by a particularly exciting idea.

ENTP

They try to seek logical explanations for every phenomena and occurrence and thrive in offering a clear explanation for it. Recognize their elaborate logical inferences if you really want to cut it with them.

ENTPs are interesting and exciting, and easy to converse with. However, owing to a penchant for logical reasoning, the discussions can get adversarial at times. They can be extremely independent and opinionated in their approach, and love to communicate with people of similar intellect.

They are precise, self-assured and confident. They go all out to keep a more objective, analytical and methodical approach towards problems and discussions. This is true even for topics related to feelings and emotions. They will analyze emotions and inner feelings.

They are active communicators and find great pleasure in exchanging opinions, concepts, critical analysis, new approaches, and ideas.

INTP

INTPs have an inherent need to categorize things for authenticating their categorizations.

As communicators, they are respectful, precise, well thought and distant. You won't find an instant warmth or cordial approach when communicating with them. However, they love to engage in logical debates with people of similar intelligence. They don't like superficial conversations, like to keep a tight social circle of like-minded folks.

They like to assess everything objectively, even while debating topics closely linked with feelings and emotions. Thus, emotional subjects don't cut it with them. Communicate with them by making critical comments about their deduced categorizations.

The SF Group

ESFJ

ESFJ people are concrete, responsive, supportive and practical in their interaction with others. They are sure of their logical reasoning and go all out to share it with others. Their communication style is softer but often assertive. They love to converse with diverse groups of people about daily affairs as well as experiences.

Refrain from bringing up very technical discussions or scientific concepts, since they are more focused on immediate, practical, workable solutions. They are great at resolving practical issues (related to management and interpersonal relationships).

ISFJ

They are friendly, thoughtful and supportive communications, who are also pragmatic and to the point. However, they take offense when their assistance or counsel is disregarded. While communicating with them, give them the impression that you appreciate and will work upon their helpful suggestions.

The ISFJ people make a great effort to build consensus for their opinion during conversations. They appreciate minding all rules and manners related to communication, and they are firm in their values.

Logical reasoning and theoretical concepts do not interest them much; hence keep discussions related to scientific concepts and technical topics to their minimum.

They typically don't have a very large social circle, which comprises mainly of people who seek to share their experiences and opinions on issues related to morality, actions, and behavior. They succeed in resolving issues in a practical and actionable manner.

ESFP

These are emotions and feelings people. It brings more meaning into their communication. They are easy communicators and find meaning in feelings. They demonstrate a sense of warmth and trust when discussing with other people. Be sincere and attentive while communicating with them. Their energy and empathy engages people and creates a lively, buzzing atmosphere.

Create a more cheerful, positive and festive atmosphere while communicating with them and you'll make the cut. They exude a deep sense of positivity and are constantly engaged in the pursuit of having open and elevated conversations that lighten the spirit. ESFP folks are more focused on finding easy and fast solutions for practical tasks that are related to building warm and fulfilling relationships.

Be more supportive, self-assured and expressive while communicating with them. Offer examples and highlight immediate advantages, benefits, and profit to help them buy into something.

ISFP

ISFPs are empathy communicators who assume the problems and pains of others as theirs. While communicating, their attention is almost always focused on various emotions. They are always keen on providing emotional support and help to other people while conversing, thus creating a more positive and good-natured interaction channel.

Again, topics that are heavily based on reasoning, logic and theoretical concepts do not make the mark where these folks are concerned. When you're trying to communicate something to them or persuade them into buying an idea, resort to feelings and emotions more than science and logic.

They enjoy sharing their feelings and frequently engage in good conversation to lighten their burden. Just don't broach topics that are too heavy, and involve a lot of technical concepts or rational arguments. They will most likely withdraw or bring the focus back to feelings and emotions in any situation. Keep it related to feelings and experiences, and you'll do well.

The NF Group

ENFJ

The ENFJ folks are blessed with exceptional communication abilities and persuasive skills that can be utilized for convincing others into their view point. They are effortless conversationalists who can quickly manage to earn people's trust. The ENFJS will happily go out of the way to offer solutions and help others.

They often lead in-depth discussions on a variety of topics and are self-assured, supportive and energetic communicators. ENFJs personality types are expressive, demonstrative and vocal about their emotions.

They find it fairly simple to communicate with other personality types on multiple topics. ENFJ people generally have a huge social circle and enjoy making new acquaintances and adding to their contacts list wherever they go.

ENFP

ENTPs often seek to understand the issues faced by others and find meaning in making others happy. This is their perception of the worlds and people around them. People's emotions have a deep impact on their spirit, and they are primary guided by the feelings. ENFPs are in their element when it comes to offering assistance and guidance to others.

Few personality types can match their capability in persuading people and inspiring their trust. They are exceptionally good at understanding, experiencing and feeling other people's feelings. The ENFP communication style is driven by their need for developing and inspiring the capabilities of other people. These guys are easy, pleasant and effortless to communicate with.

They abhor monotony, which is reflected in their communication patterns, where they take on in-depth discussions about a huge variety of subjects. Their communication patterns also are diversified to suit different people, which makes it easy for them to communicate with other personality types. They offer to start stimulating discussions, though they have an inherent dislike for heavily analytical topics.

INFJ

Similar to folks in the other NF group, INFJ people derive great pleasure in helping others even in seemingly impossible situations. It offers their existence more meaning and motivation.

Their communication style is more caring, thoughtful, empathetic and supportive. Communicating with this group becomes fairly easy if you focus more on feelings and emotions. Be pleasant, easy and attentive while communicating with them since their inherent disposition is more easy-going.

However, they can appear more standoffish and reserved in their communication. They take time to collect their emotions, events, and thoughts. The INFJ circle social circle isn't very extensive. It consists of a close-knit group of family, friends, and acquaintances.

Be expressive, utilize visual aids, and appeal to their intuition if you want to communicate effectively with them. Throw them challenges and watch them thrive. Rather than focusing on the current problem, try and bring their attention to the bigger picture.

INFP

An INFPs view of things around them is established by notions of right and wrong, and fair and unfair. They are in their element when they think they are doing the fair and right thing.

Few personality types can match their ability to empathize with people and sense people's concerns. They possess an inherent knack for being able to inspire other people's talents and skills. INFPs are capable of offering emotional support to those around them, and hence should be communicated with on a more feeling based and intuitive level. Relate to their spiritual, intuitive side, and you'll win their trust.

Their social circle comprises a large number of people, and their communication patterns can be intense. People are often interested in soliciting their expert opinion on a variety of subjects. They generally prefer communicating through a mass medium than addressing people individually.

Their communication style involves inner feelings related to the soul and all things spiritual. When the discussion is more esoteric conceptual in nature, they find it easy to have a meaningful conversation.

It's easier for INFPs to connect with people who share a more intuitive or feeling type of mindset. If you want to have common ground with them, focus less on reasoning and more on feelings. Their discussion or communication pattern is focused on a more creative and less theoretical nature.

Conclusion

Thank you for choosing the book, How to Analyze People. I sincerely hope it has provided you several proven strategies, foolproof tips and effective techniques for analyzing people in different situations and settings of life, and made you the ultimate people reader!

Whether you're trying to gauge what a potential client is thinking during negotiations or your hot new date is sufficiently attracted to you or if you're hiring the right person, this book presents several practical tips and wisdom nuggets to help you read people like books in all walks of life – even when they don't talk much!

The next step is to simply use this valuable resource by applying in your everyday life. You aren't going to be an FBI style accurate people analyzer in a day. It will come with lots of observation, practice, and application. Learn to get into the habit of observing and analyzing people using these techniques in varied settings from supermarkets to airports to cafes, when you have some time at hand.

Here's to being a fantastic people analyzer, who can use the power of reading people's thoughts and feelings to transform lives!

Cognitive Behavioral Therapy

Master Your Brain, Depression And Anxiety

Includes Effective Self-Help Cognitive Behavioral Techniques

Written by

George Muntau

Chapter One:

Understanding Anxiety and Depression

To gain a comprehensive and well-rounded understanding of CBT or cognitive behavioral therapy, we must first take a close look at depression and anxiety. What exactly constitutes depression? This is especially relevant because people tend to use the term loosely to indicate an unhappy mindset. Haven't you heard people drop the term depression ever so often when they are having a bad day or simply in a low mood?

Depression as a mental condition is far graver than we believe. It is a state where an individual suffering from it feels melancholic, hopeless, demotivated and discouraged. There is a general sense of disinterest about life. If this feeling doesn't last for long, it may simply be a case of "feeling the blues" when one feels low. However, if these feelings assume a chronic and continuous pattern (so much so that it interferes with your personal and professional life), there may be a serious clinical issue at hand.

Typically, when the condition lasts for over two weeks and when these depressive feelings interfere with your everyday tasks such as looking after the family, fulfilling professional responsibilities, going out with friends or studying, it is likely to be a considerable depressive condition or episode.

Depression is a widely prevalent mental condition in the United States. In 2014 alone, 15.7 million adults (above 18) experienced a minimum of one depression episode in the span of a year. At any given point, 3 to 5 percent of adult Americans suffer from significantly major depression. Not just adults, about 2 out of every 100 young children and about 8 out of 100 teenagers suffer from depression.

The overall picture related to depression is not so grim after all. It is a treatable condition that can change the way an individual thinks, experiences, feels, acts and functions in day to day life.

Though depression can occur at any age, it usually begins at the onset of adulthood. It is also observed in children and adolescents in the form of irritability, a low feeling or extreme mood swings. The roots of chronic mood swings, depression or anxiety disorders can be traced back to the increased anxiety we experienced as children.

It can also occur during your midlife or old age due to serious physical or medical ailments such as cancer, Parkinson's, heart diseases and diabetes. These conditions can trigger depressive tendencies or can worsen an already existing condition of depression. Sometimes depression can be a side effect of medications used to treat these ailments.

What Causes Depression?

Though the exact cause of depression isn't known, there are a number of factors (often interlinked) that can lead to depressive episodes or chronic depression. It often results from a number of recent events or long-term factors rather than a single incident or event. It is strongly rooted in a person's early psychological development or experiences, and how they come together with an immediate event or incident.

It is believed to be caused by a combination of genetic, environmental, psychological, and biological factors. It will vary from individual to individual depending on which factor takes precedence over others. However, as a general framework, depression can be largely attributed to these factors.

For instance, some who have had a relatively healthy psychological development and favorable early childhood experiences will be better equipped to cope with a negative immediate experience than a person who struggles with self-esteem or his/her emotions. Thus, the second person is likelier to suffer from depression in the absence of a strong psychological development. Thus, depression is not an immediate consequence of something that has happened recently. It is more of a combination of a person's psychological health in response to something that has happened recently.

Negative Life Events

Studies have pointed to the fact that continuing or prolonged challenges in life invariably lead to depression in people with less evolved coping abilities. This can be persistent unemployment, being in an abusive or apathetic relationship, prolonged isolation or even continuous work-related stress.

Thus, it is a prolonged state of events rather than immediate events that are likely to cause depression. Of course, immediate events can trigger or launch depression when a person is already in a high state of risk due to unfavorable experiences or multiple personal issues.

Family History

Depression can also be a genetic condition. You may be at a higher genetic risk of suffering from depression if it runs in the family or someone in the family suffers from it.

However, don't automatically assume that just because someone in the family has struggled with depression, you'll get it too. There are plenty of other factors involved that are related to the person's circumstances, early childhood experiences, personal factors and psychological framework.

Grave Medical Illness

Increased stress, uncertainty and worry about coping with a grave illness can cause depressive tendencies. This is especially true for people who have to deal with a long-term illness, chronic pain or low chances of survival.

Individual Personality

A person's personality determines to a large extent whether or not he/she is likely to suffer from depression or the extent to which external circumstances can affect him/her and lead to depressive tendencies.

If your personality is more prone towards pessimism, worry, and low self-esteem, you may be at a higher risk of being affected negatively. Some people are inherently sensitive towards criticism, have a higher tendency to worry and are extremely self-critical. They may be at a higher risk of being impacted by what others say or unfavorable situations.

People who sport a less sensitive personality, are more self-confident and generally feature a more optimistic/positive personality are less likely to be negatively impacted by their circumstances. This approach makes them less prone to depression.

Substance or Alcohol Abuse

Depression can be a direct consequence of alcohol or drug abuse. When there is excessive dependence on an external object for "feeling good," there are major issues related to self-esteem and personality.

It can also be the other way around. Depression can also lead to substance or alcohol abuse since, at the root, the causes of both are almost interwoven. People often resort to drugs or alcohol as a means of escaping one reality, which is a strong trigger for depression.

Chemical Changes in the Brain

This is a slightly gray area where causes of depression are concerned because there isn't any conclusive research to back the premise.

It's not as simple as excessive or not enough brain chemicals. There are a large number of factors such as genetic pattern, extreme life stressors, medications/substances consumed over a period of time and medical conditions that may have impacted the way our brain controls our moods or feelings.

Many contemporary antidepressants are known to impact our brain's chemical makeup. They have a direct bearing on the secretion of noradrenaline and serotonin that pass messages from brain cells. This is how they are effective when it comes to treating depression along with psychological techniques such as CBT.

Types of Depression

Clinical depression disorders can be primarily classified into three major types – persistent depression disorder, major depression and bipolar disorder.

Persistent Depression Disorder

Persistent Depression Disorder is a type of depression that generally lasts for a minimum of two years. Though it isn't as severe as major depression, the symptoms are almost similar.

The individual experiences low energy, a lackluster appetite (or binge eating episodes), sleeplessness or being in a state of inactivity. It can reveal itself in the form of exhaustion, stress, irritability or anhedonia (the state of being unable to gain pleasure from a majority of activities). People suffering from PDD tend to have a more pessimistic view of life, and focus on their "half empty glass."

Major Depression

Major depression lasts continuously for at least weeks. The episode is majorly disabling and constantly interferes with an individual's ability to fulfill his/her every responsibility such as eating, managing a home, working, caring for others and sleeping. Generally, major depression bouts occur about once or twice in a person's lifetime. However, it can be more frequent in some cases.

Major depression can also be the direct result of a sudden, extreme situation such as the death of a loved one, end of a relationship, illness or another major life event. It may not be so much about the event as it is about the individual's inability to cope with the event. In extreme cases, the person does not think that there's anything in life worth living for, which leads them to take their own lives.

Bipolar Disorder

Bipolar disorder is nothing but manic depression characterized by extreme mood swings and cycles that go from severely high (often known as mania) to mild high (called hypomania) to extremely low (depression).

During a mania episode, an individual usually experiences particularly elevated or high feelings. There is a general sense of irritation, an inability to sleep, ideas of grandiose, excessive talking, fast moving thoughts, elevated desire for sex, a clear increase in energy, faulty judgment, and unsuitable social behavior.

During the low or depression phase, the person experiences symptoms similar to major depression. The mood shifts from manic elevation to depressive lows are often gradual, though at times they can also be extremely abrupt or immediate.

Symptoms of Depression

If you are experiencing these symptoms or physical/psychological patterns almost daily or a major part of the day or for over two weeks, there may be a possibility you are suffering from depressive tendencies. Here are some symptoms of depression.

1. A persistent feeling of sorrow or emptiness
2. An increased or abnormal feeling of pessimism about everything around you
3. High feeling of irritability
4. Feeling of guilt, regret, worthlessness, low self-esteem and helplessness
5. Loss of interest in pleasurable activities, interests or hobbies

6. Low energy, exhaustion or fatigue

7. Speaking, walking or moving slowly

8. Feeling increasingly restless or finding it challenging to sit or lay still

9. Having trouble focusing, retaining/recalling information or wielding decisions

10. Having trouble sleeping or oversleeping

11. Sudden changes in appetite or weight

12. Negative thoughts related to suicide, death or suicidal attempts, a persistent feeling of hopelessness or that life isn't worth living

13. Physical aches or pains, headache, body cramps or persistent digestive issues without any clear or apparent physical condition/cause, which doesn't decrease with medication or treatment.

Bear in mind that not everyone who suffers from depression will experience all these symptoms or signs. You may only experience some of these depending on the factors leading to depression or the type of depression. The severity, duration, and frequency of these symptoms will help your medical practitioner diagnose the exact condition.

Treatment and Therapies

The good news like I stated earlier is that even in its most severe form, depression can be generally treated. The sooner you start treatment, the higher your chances of coming out of the condition.

Depression is generally treated with one or a combination of these, depending on the severity of the condition – medication, psychotherapy or both. If these treatments are not effective or do not produce the desired results, electroconvulsive therapy (ECT) or other stimulation based therapies can be considered.

The most important thing to keep in mind is that unlike other ailments, there's no "one-size-fits-all" line of treatment for depression since rarely will two individuals suffer from depression in the same manner. It may take multiple treatments and some amount of trial and error to figure out the most effective line of treatment for a person.

Medicines

Antidepressants have proven to be effective in treating some forms of depression. They can be helpful in managing the way your brain processes specific chemicals to influence your mood, emotions or stress. The practitioner may prescribe multiple anti-depressants to find the one that best mitigates your symptoms and features minimal or non-intrusive side effects.

Medicines usually take a fortnight or a month to show noticeable results and minimize symptoms. Antidepressants can help you improve your appetite, increase concentration and bring about a slight mood lift.

One of the most important things to consider before taking any antidepressant for depression is that it should never be taken without consulting a doctor. Just because a friend benefitted from it doesn't mean you'll automatically experience the same relief or effectiveness.

As discussed above, every case of depression varies, and the line of treatment depends on the individual's unique condition. Also, it isn't advisable to stop medication without a doctor's consent, since there are high chances of it returning.

In several instances, people discontinue medication when they start feeling better.

However, it usually takes about 6 to 12 months for the symptoms to reduce. Your medical practitioner will gradually decrease the dose depending on your condition. Stopping them suddenly can lead to withdrawal symptoms, which can worsen the symptoms/condition.

Psychotherapy

Psychotherapy or talk therapy can also be used to treat people suffering from depression. Specific therapies that are known to be effective in treating depression include Cognitive Behavioral Therapy, Interpersonal Therapy, and Problem-Solving Therapy.

Brain Stimulation Therapy

When medications and other therapies do not mitigate depression symptoms, doctors may suggest an electroconvulsive therapy (ECT). It is especially helpful for people suffering from prolonged and severe depression, who haven't found much success with other forms of treatment. In some instances, when a quick response is needed, or medications have failed to yield the desired effect, ECT is adopted as an intervention. Typically, ECT sessions are performed twice or thrice a week for about three to four weeks.

Anxiety

Anxiety is increased fear, nervousness or panic. Though the feeling of anxiousness is common in people at different points in time (think of your first job interview or first date), in anxiety, it is more than normal. All of us worry about something at various points in life. However, this cannot be termed as a chronic case of anxiety or anxiety related disorder. If the problem or challenging situation has long disappeared, but you still experience anxiety, it may be a red flag.

People experience a usual sense of fear, worry or nervousness before tackling any challenging or important event in life such as a crucial examination, speaking in front of an audience, a public recital or job interview. An increased feeling of fear, uncertainty, and nervousness in the above-mentioned scenario is considered fair. It becomes a disorder only when it interferes with an individual's ability to lead a normal life, sleep or perform everyday tasks.

When the reaction to a given situation is totally out of proportion or magnified, it can be a case of anxiety disorder. For instance, while it is normal to be slightly nervous or scared during a job interview, breaking into a sweat or experiencing excessive fear each time you are introduced to a person/stranger may point to a case of anxiety. The reaction in the latter case is not promotional to the external stimuli.

One out of every six youngsters suffers from anxiety issues at some point. It is a fairly common disorder, which can be controlled with the right line of treatment.

Symptoms of Anxiety

- Experiencing fear, nervousness and a sense of panic most of the time
- A general feeling of despair or depression
- Loss of appetite
- Inability to concentrate
- Insomnia
- An overwhelming feeling of irritability, tiredness, and exhaustion
- Increased palpitations

- Dryness in the mouth

- Trembling and shaking with fear or nervousness

- Feeling weak or faint

- Cramps in the stomach/intestine and/or frequent motions

Again, if you have some of these or even all of these symptoms, it doesn't automatically signal anxiety. You have to have a diagnosis from a medical practitioner to ascertain that the condition is indeed anxiety.

Types of Anxiety Disorders

Anxiety disorders can be categorized into multiple specific disorders. Some of the most prevalent ones are –

General Anxiety Disorder

General Anxiety Disorder or GAD is nothing but a chronic disorder that comprises of increased, longer durations of anxiety, nervousness, and worry not related to any specific events, things and situations. It's a feeling of excessive worry without any clear cause to worry.

People who suffer from general anxiety often fall prey to worrying about their loved ones, work, school, health, finances, etc. However, they are unable to identify a clear and precise cause for the worry. The fear is generally unfounded, impractical and out of proportion or not in sync with the expected response to the situation.

Those who suffer from general anxiety expect disaster, failure and negative outcomes to an extent that it interferes with their daily functions like relationships, social pursuits, and professional responsibilities.

Panic Disorder

Panic Disorder is a kind of anxiety which involves sudden, abrupt attacks of extreme terror, fear or apprehension that result in dizziness, a confused state of mind, violent shaking and dryness of the mouth. It can also cause trouble in breathing and a feeling of nausea. Panic attacks typically keep rising and reach their peak in 10 minutes. However, they can last for several hours.

Often a result of some frightening experiences, it can also occur due to extended periods of stress, though spontaneous panic attacks are not uncommon.

Panic attacks lead people to be excessively sensitive to any changes in the body or health and interpret them as life threatening (hypochondriasis). They also expect these attacks in future thus leading to the drastic changes in their behavior pattern in anticipation of panic attacks.

Phobias

Phobia is irrational or unfounded fear of any object, person or situation. It differs from general anxiety in the sense that the extreme response is related to a clear cause or specific stimuli. The fear is often known to be irrational, out of proportion or unnecessary. However, the person can't help in controlling his/her anxiety that directly results from the particular stimuli.

Social Anxiety Disorder

Social anxiety disorder is a kind of social phobia mainly characterized by excessive fear of not being accepted or being negatively judged by people, which can lead to public embarrassment. It includes everything from stage fear to fear of developing interpersonal relationships to a clear fear of being humiliated in public.

The disorder can acquire such an extreme magnitude that it can cause the person suffering from social anxiety disorder to stop participating in social gatherings or completely avoiding any human contact which causes a breakdown in everyday tasks.

Obsessive Compulsive Disorder (OCD)

Obsessive Compulsive Disorder (OCD) is an anxiety related disorder involving intrusive thoughts, behavior patterns or actions. They are repetitive, stressful and intrusive to the point of interfering with everyday functions. People who suffer from OCD are pretty much aware that their compulsions are illogical and incoherent, but they still succumb to it in order to get rid of their anxiety.

They may insist on walking in a specific pattern, wash their hands multiple times during the day, check if things have been arranged in a particular order several times or display other similar behavior patterns (checking locks or light switches). People suffering from OCD can also be victims of obsessive, intrusive thoughts, which may interfere with their everyday functions.

Post-Traumatic Stress Disorder

Post-Traumatic Stress Disorder is a type of anxiety that results directly from a traumatic event such as sexual violence, military combat, being held hostage, a grave accident, and other similar situations. Rather than being founded on psychological conditions over a period of time, it is based on a single, unfortunate event that has serious repercussions on one's psyche. It causes flashbacks, changes in one's behavior and general manner of living based on avoiding specific stimuli.

Separation Anxiety Disorder

Separation Anxiety Disorder is when a person experiences increased levels of anxiety owing to separation from a particular place or person, so much so that their sense of security and safety is shaken. The separation can also lead to panic at times and assumes the form of a disorder when the reaction is extreme, irrational or inappropriate.

Anxiety Treatment

Much like depression, anxiety disorders can also be treated using several methods including therapy and medication. The specific line of treatment will vary according to the nature and magnitude of the disorder.

However, anxiety disorders, in general, can be treated with medication, therapy, and in some instances a combination of both.

Therapy

Cognitive Behavioral Therapy can be used to treat anxiety related disorders like panic attacks, general anxiety, and phobias. Cognitive Behavioral therapy emphasizes on thoughts or cognitive patterns and behavior. As a line of treatment for anxiety, it helps identify/recognize and tackle negative thought patterns and unfounded ideas that trigger the anxiety.

Exposure therapy in anxiety disorder urges people to confront or tackle their fears in a more secure and controlled set-up. Through frequent exposure of the object or circumstance (in reality or state of imagination), there is a more efficient control mechanism. As one faces their fear unharmed, the anxiety slowly decreases.

Cognitive behavioral therapy and exposure therapy are both behavioral therapies, which means they rely solely on a person's behavior than underlying emotional conflicts or early childhood experiences.

Medication

If you are suffering from an extreme anxiety disorder that interferes with your everyday functions, your doctor may prescribe medications to help decrease the symptoms. There can be some side effects of taking medicines to treat anxiety; however, it is also known to be effective in mitigating the condition over a period of time. It is best to let a medical practitioner diagnose the disorder correctly, and employ the most effective line of treatment depending on your individual condition. There are multiple self-help techniques that can be used to treat anxiety disorders effectively minus the negative side-effects.

Difference Between Anxiety and Depression

The relationship between various mental disorders can be convoluted. There is no error-proof way of determining whether a person is suffering from anxiety or depression. Both can be present in an individual simultaneously (often referred to medically as a comorbid issue). Or, one can cause the other.

For instance, a person can lapse into a state of depression owing to his/her anxiety disorder. Symptoms of one disorder may easy overlap another, making it challenging to determine the exact disorder an individual is suffering from.

Since depression and anxiety share similar causes, symptoms and treatment methods, it can be tough to tell them apart.

Though the symptoms of both conditions are almost the same, anxiety is more related to feelings of apprehension about the future. It is a persistent worry or nervousness about something going wrong. There is a great need to escape or avoid certain things, or situations that can cause anxiety.

Depression, on the other hand, is a feeling of sadness, despair or hopelessness. There is a general feeling of listlessness (not worry unlike anxiety). People suffering from anxiety often suffer from worry about something negative happening to them in future, while people with depression assume that there is nothing positive about their life and that their future is doomed.

The physical symptoms can also vary slightly, though there are some similarities. Both conditions can leave you feeling stressed, exhausted and low on energy physically. While in anxiety, this can happen after an instance of intense anxiety, in depression, it can be a more persistent physical state, minus any real immediate triggers.

Anxiety triggers reveal more flight or escape type of reactions such as excessive sweating, an increased need to run or terrible shaking. The heart rate increases dramatically, accompanied by hyperventilation. In depression, there is a major lack of enthusiasm, drive, passion or energy. There's a lack of feelings or emotions, and slowed thoughts, decisions, and actions. Depression also involves severe changes in one's appetite, while causing chronic headaches, eating disorders and erratic sleep patterns. There is an overwhelming sense of sadness and negativity.

Depression has much fewer physical symptoms than anxiety. However, its mental signs or symptoms are so overpowering that they can affect physical functions, and in extreme cases lead to suicidal tendencies. Depression can very well be a secondary condition of anxiety or an aftermath of anxiety attacks.

Chapter Two:

Decoding Cognitive Behavioral Therapy

Cognitive behavioral therapy (CBT) is a relatively short-term, results-oriented type of psychotherapy, which has a clear goal and uses a more practical approach for tackling psychological disorders. The goal usually is to change behavior or thought patterns that cause people to feel the way they do. CBT is employed for treating a large number of mental ailments or disorders from insomnia to relationship issues to substance abuse or anxiety/depression.

The therapy involves altering an individual's behavior patterns and attitude by concentrating on their thoughts, visual imagery, underlying beliefs and overall attitude (held in the person's cognizance), and impacting the way it processes a person's behavior and manner of dealing with psychological problems.

One of the biggest benefits of cognitive behavior therapy is that it is a short-term remedy, often taking not more than five to nine months for a majority of psychological issues. The sessions typically last for about 40-550 minutes and are conducted once a week. During the CBT sessions, clients and therapists work in unison to identify the underlying cause of the problem and to develop novel techniques for dealing with it. It seeks to introduce individuals to strategies that can be applied throughout their life.

Cognitive behavioral therapy is considered a holistic combination of both behavioral therapy and psychotherapy. While psychotherapy focuses on the significance or the relevance of our early childhood in our thinking and behavioral patterns, behavioral therapy emphasizes on the close equation between our psychological problems, behavior patterns, and thoughts.

CBT relies on the premise that the manner in which we think or our cognition abilities, the manner in which we experience feelings, or our emotional abilities determine our behavior and influence each other. For instance, our thoughts lead us to behave in a particular manner. If we feel threatened by something, our behavior immediately reflects the need to escape from that situation or thing.

Cognitive behavioral therapy combines psychotherapy and behavior therapy by placing focus on the individual meaning we assign to things and our thought processes that can be traced to early childhood experiences. Behavioral therapy focuses on the connection between the challenges we face and our actions and thoughts. A majority of the psychotherapists who employ CBT personalize the therapy to suit the individual needs of every patient.

Negative and unpleasant thoughts can often lead to emotional distress and result in psychological issues. When a person struggles with emotional distress, his/her interpretation of various situations becomes distorted, thus triggering negative behavior or actions.

Cognitive behavioral therapy attempts to assist people to gain a better awareness of their negative interpretation and behavioral patterns, which arise from skewed thinking. Cognitive therapy helps in developing several alternate ways of processing our thoughts and actions to mitigate psychological trauma.

CBT focuses on identifying an issue, challenging it head on and changing the way we view a particular situation. It is like we perceive the world in a particular manner. CBT seeks to make us aware of how our thought patterns lead to the creation of our reality and influence our behavior.

CBT – A Background

Cognitive behavioral therapy was originally created about half a decade ago for treating chronic depression. Today it is widely used for treating a string of mental and behavioral disorders such as anxiety, post-traumatic stress disorder, panic attacks, social phobia, bipolar disorder, obsessive compulsive disorder, substance abuse, schizophrenia, eating disorders, anger issues and similar other challenging conditions.

The therapy was founded by psychiatrist Aron Beck in the 60s. He had undertaken a research on psychoanalysis and noted that during these sessions, patients demonstrated a tendency for having an internal dialogue or thought process. It came across like they were trying to have a conversation with themselves. However, when inquired, they wouldn't reveal much of this internal dialogue to the therapist.

Beck is known to be one of the founders of the cognitive focused therapies. Albert Ellis was the creator of conventional cognitive therapies. He also underlined the importance of cognitions or thinking of our feelings and reactions. When we talk about CBT, we are in essence referring to both Dr. Beck's Cognitive Behavioral Therapy and Dr. Elli's Rational Emotive

Behavior Therapy along with much other thought and behavior oriented therapies.

It dawned upon Beck gradually that the connection between feelings/emotions and thoughts was crucial. He came up with the concept of automatic thoughts or thoughts that are the result of the immediate emotions we experience.

Beck discovered that people are not always aware of their emotion laden thoughts, though they are capable of identifying and mentioning these thoughts. For instance, if a person felt upset, his/her thought pattern was generally negative, destructive and impractical. It soon became evident to Beck that an individual's thoughts played a huge role in comprehending and overcoming his/her challenges.

It was termed cognitive therapy initially because of the emphasis on thoughts. Behavioral was later added to the therapy because it started incorporating various behavioral techniques too. The proportion of thoughts and behavior varies from therapy to therapy depending on the condition; however, they all come in the bracket of cognitive behavioral therapy. Since its inception, CBT has undergone intensive research and trials by various psychological experts for a range of mental health issues.

Beck elaborated that the view and interpretations of people who suffer from depression and other mental health issues are distorted. These individuals are likelier to experience cognitive errors that make them prone to negative thinking, catastrophizing, and processing extreme thoughts.

Beck realized that our skewed thinking process was more a result of automatic, involuntary thoughts, and our tendency to accept these distorted thoughts as the truth. CBT emphasizes on transforming our automatic and spontaneous thoughts by questioning their validity as opposed to reality. When a person halts their destructive, catastrophic and self-critical thinking, their sense of despair and worry gradually decreases, and they are able to live a more positive and fulfilled life.

Recent studies have suggested that cognitive behavioral therapy is more effective than medication in treating some conditions such as insomnia. The beauty of the therapy is that it can be used for just about any maladjusted behavior, where thoughts and ideas play a crucial role.

Three Major Approaches to Cognitive Behavioral Therapy

Rational Emotive Behavior Therapy

The rational emotive behavior therapy seeks to amend maladaptive thoughts, faulty thinking patterns of the patient. It utilizes persuasion and discussion for helping clients alter their thought process.

Beck's Cognitive Therapy

The therapy was initially founded by Aron Beck for treating depression but later went on to encompass other conditions such as anxiety and eating disorders. It is now also widely used for tackling fatigue syndromes and chronic stress. The focus is on increasing the patient's awareness and the link between thought processes and subsequent emotional responses. Patients are trained to recognize their involuntary or automatic thoughts.

Stress Inoculation Therapy

Stress Inoculation therapy comprises of self-guided training that emphasizes on self-transformational statements or affirmations. It's like giving yourself a nice pep-talk to alter your thoughts and subsequent actions.

Cognitive-Behavioral Intervention Examples

Take for instance a person who approaches his therapist with issues related to low self-confidence or self-esteem. The therapist will first recognize his involuntary negative thoughts termed as cognitive distortions. These are nothing but our distorted version of reality. It is damaging because it's automatic, almost like a reflex. It is so deeply ingrained in our subconscious that we believe it to be true.

In the above example, a person's view of himself may be highly skewed or distorted due to early childhood experiences or life events. He may operate from the perspective that he's worthless or not good enough to do anything.

The stage where the therapist attempts to understand an individual's thought patterns is termed as functional analysis. Together the client and therapist work in recognizing these automatic thought patterns, and replacing it with more constructive or positive thoughts chosen by both, such as "I am of tremendous value" or "there are several things I do really well."

A woman is finding it challenging to enjoy a fulfilling interpersonal relationship with her husband owing to the fact that he doesn't spend enough time with her. With assistance from the therapist, the woman can discover that her feelings that her husband doesn't love her or is indifferent to her are unfounded.

The therapist attempts to ask her if she believes this to be real. The thought that her husband doesn't love her is challenged. This destructive thought is then replaced with a more constructive alternative idea that "my husband loves me of course; he is only busy creating a better future for my children and me."

A man is slowly recovering from alcohol addiction and is closely working with a therapist to recognize high-risk triggers that stimulate his impulse for drinking. Together they come up with a list of strategies that help overcome or tackle these overpowering impulses.

The client implements and rehearses these coping techniques. For instance, avoiding a social situation where the urge for drinking is likely to be triggered or using a series of relaxation methods like meditation and yoga. Therapists may come up with strategies that mentally distract the client or substitute the strong impulse for drinking with another less destructive behavior.

Chapter Three:

Dealing With Intrusive Thoughts

CBT is based on the premise that it isn't the situation or circumstances that cause the condition, but the meaning assigned to these situations that lead us to experience depression or anxiety. The way we interpret a particular situation is what makes us slip into a negative state of mind. Often, the ideas that we hold about events or situations are impractical or blown out of proportion.

When these misleading notions are not challenged, they continue to grow stronger and lead to even more negativity. We assume it as our reality, which blocks us from perceiving things as they are and leading a fulfilling life. There is a tendency to overlook or ignore things that do not match our negative perception of events and situations. We continue to let these thoughts grow unhindered.

For instance, a person suffering from depression will think that he/she just can't go to the office today because nothing's going to be positive. Their thoughts operate from a sense of hopelessness. They end up believing what they think is true.

So according to the person, nothing positive is bound to happen at work today, which means with their negative thought pattern there's absolutely no opportunity of knowing if this feeling is right or wrong. The person doesn't give himself/herself a chance to ascertain the veracity of their claims. Their thinking itself leads to the negative or unpleasant experience.

In the above example, the person stays at home and doesn't go to work. Thus he/she doesn't know whether their negative prediction had any clear basis. Such individuals sit at home thinking that they are an absolute failure and that they've let people down. They become angry with themselves and think about how incompetent and useless they are. This leads to the person feeling even worse than earlier, which results in more difficulty while attending office the following day. This causes a downward thinking, behavior and feeling spiral or a vicious circle that leads to several problems.

Where Do The Thoughts Originate?

According to the founder of CBT Aron Beck, the thoughts can be traced back to our childhood, when they become relatively rigid and involuntary. For instance, a child who may not have got enough attention and affection from the family but was encouraged to perform well academically may grow up with the notion that people have to be a success or do well every time. Such individuals will start believing that if they are not successful, people won't accept them. This may lead to the person putting excessive pressure on himself and slipping into depression if he fails to meet their own standards for success.

They may not experience the desired success due to something that's beyond their realm of control, which triggers the negative or dysfunctional thought. The person may believe that he/she isn't good enough or is a total failure. This will lead them to think they won't be accepted by others, and hence withdraw socially.

Cognitive behavioral therapy helps people to gain awareness of the fact that their mind is processing thoughts in a more skewed manner. It assists them in stepping out of their involuntary thought pattern and challenges these unfounded thoughts.

In the above instance, it challenges the person to assess her real-life instances for determining whether her thoughts are in congruence with reality. If something that has happened in their past or to someone else has indeed matched their perspective about the situation.

This helps them gain a greater realistic perspective, and they may end up gaining an opportunity to test the perspectives of other people by revealing their situation to close friends and family members.

There's no denying that negative things happen. However, when we are in a tough state of mind, our perspective and interpretations operate from a more biased plane. Thus we magnify the challenge we face. CBT assists people in modifying these skewed interpretations and helps them see things from a more balanced perspective.

CBT for Intrusive OCD Thoughts

Cognitive behavioral therapy points out that OCD or Obsessive Compulsive Disorder is when people misread intrusive thoughts or compelling urges as indications that harm will occur and they are directly responsible for their actions.

When it comes to treating OCD or intrusive thoughts through CBT, it helps individuals understand that their intrusive or disturbing obsessive thoughts are nothing but a result of anxiety than any real danger. OCD patients are gradually made to realize that they won't be affected or in danger if they don't give in to these thoughts.

People with OCD are desperately trying to avoid harm. Their solutions invariably end up becoming part of the issue. For instance, if you keep thinking about neutralizing your thoughts about stabbing someone, it only ends up increasing these intrusive thoughts.

The real issues, therefore, aren't these intrusive thoughts but the meaning assigned to them by an individual suffering from OCD. For example, you may experience a huge urge to act upon your intrusive thoughts or that you shouldn't have these thoughts in the first place. This places a huge level of threat, anxiety, and responsibility on you. In the above example, you'll stop meeting the person alone or stop stocking your kitchen with knives. You've succumbed to the fear. The fear is still alive, and further stops you from thinking that your fear is nothing but a skewed thought.

One of the most important aspects of using CBT to treat OCD or intrusive thoughts is that the therapist only functions as a facilitator and that it has to be practiced on your own.

Different therapists focus on different cognitive and behavioral attributes of OCD or intrusive thoughts. A cognitive focused approach will help you assess your thought patterns more keenly. For instance, you have thoughts about killing someone, which makes you feel that are a bad person for having these thoughts and you could act upon them. Your therapist will work with you to seek a different understanding of these distorted thoughts and give you an alternate technique for reacting to them.

If it's a more behavioral focused approach, it could be focused on educating yourself about how anxiety is felt by the body. It is about facing your fears and gradually taking on, and increasing the very activities you fear. For instance, if you suffer from social anxiety, your therapist will slowly get you to come out of your shell and participate in interactions on a smaller scale.

Where OCD or intrusive thoughts are concerned, the end goal of CBT is to change the brain's thought process or structure. Even if this sounds like a Herculean task, it isn't. Let's consider an example.

Let's assume you have lived in the United States of America all your life, and are used to a right-hand drive. There was no hassle of changing gears. Suddenly, you have to move to the United Kingdom, which is a left-hand drive. How will you manage?

To learn to drive left-handed, you have to unlearn right-handed driving. What makes the entire pursuit tough is that it has become a subconscious or almost involuntary process. If you've never driven left-handed, you'll initially have trouble getting used to sides, looking in the wrong direction and stepping out.

However, once you change or alter your actions and gradually get used to driving left-handed, you will learn to drive in the new direction. It comes with exposure, practice, and repetition. Repeated left handed driving experiences help you navigate corners, look in the right direction and step out with confidence. You practice this repeatedly until you've altered your brain structure.

Similarly, CBT seeks to question the veracity of your intrusive thoughts by consistent action, thus leading to a change in thought patterns. It transforms unrealistic and impractical intrusive thoughts into more real and evidence focused patterns. CBT will also help you restructure your behavior about avoiding certain things that lead to intrusive thoughts.

For instance, if you experience repetitive thoughts about wanting to stab someone, you overcome avoiding holding knives or being alone with the person. Over a period of time, repeated new experiences help your brain learn to control anxiety experienced as a result of these irrational thoughts.

Cognitive Distortions

Cognitive distortions as the name suggest are thoughts or pattern of thinking that leads us to believe something that is not true. When you identify that you hold misleading or untrue cognitive perceptions or thoughts, it is easier to balance it with more rational thoughts. Here are some of the most common cognitive distortions.

Polarization

This type of cognitive distortion involves perceiving everything in extremes, with no balanced or gray thinking. This is an all or nothing thought pattern that doesn't have any scope for considering more balanced or complex behavioral nuances. For instance, if you don't perform perfectly in one aspect of work, you may consider yourself to be a total professional failure rather than being unskilled in a specific area.

Filtering

Filtering refers to the several ways through which we completely ignore all the positive aspects about a particular thing and emphasize only on the negative. In this form of cognitive distortion, it becomes almost involuntary to focus on a single damaging aspect despite being surrounded by positive things.

Personalization

This is a sort of cognitive distortion where a person thinks that every of his action has a direct bearing on his external circumstances and other individuals, no matter how illogical it seems. The link may be completely unreasonable; however, he ends up believing that everything bad that happens to him was his fault.

For example, when a person suffers from excessive personalization, he believes that the meeting turned out to be an absolute disaster because he was a couple of minutes late.

This is sort of assuming responsibility or blaming oneself for everything that goes wrong.

Overgeneralization

Overgeneralization is taking an isolated incident, occurrence or thing and making it the only piece of evidence for making sweeping conclusions. For example, a person may have been cheated in a romantic relationship once, and she turns down romantic relationships in the future stating that everyone is a cheat and no one is worth getting into a relationship with.

Similarly, if a person has had an unpleasant experience at a job interview once, he will make sweeping generalizations that he is terrible at job interviews, and won't find a job ever again. Stray incidents are believed to be a general reality, even in the face of evidence suggesting otherwise.

Blaming

When something doesn't happen according to the way a person wants, they resort to assigning the responsibility for the outcome on someone else. There is an excessive need to blame other people for making us act, feel or think in a particular manner. Our feelings and actions are often a result of our own perceptions, and hence blaming others for what we feel or how we behave is nothing but a type of distortion.

Catastrophizing

This distortion has to do with anticipating the worst in any given situation, based on something that is not comparable in magnitude to what the person is actually imagining. A good example is when a person injures his toe and imagines that he may die soon based solely on a small injury. There is no logical connection between what has actually happened and what he imagined.

Similarly, the person may make a small mistake at work, and imagine that her boss will sack her. There is also a tendency to minimize positive accomplishments. In the above example, the person will overlook rewards and recognition gained at work and focus solely on the error (imagining unreasonable consequences).

Global Labeling

This is again a type of generalization where the person picks single instances or attributes and passes more global judgment. For instance, if we don't do a task particularly well or do not have the requisite skill to fulfill a particular task, we end up labeling ourselves total failures. We apply what may be good in one area in several other areas.

Similarly, when someone says something slightly rude, we jump to the conclusion that he/she is a terrible person. Mislabeling is all about exaggerated, emotionally wrought and irrational labels that are assigned to a particular situation. Think a woman who has gone out with her friends, leaving her children in the care of their babysitter. A person suffering from global labeling will term this as the woman dumping her children or not caring about them.

Control Fallacies

There is a tendency to feel that everything that happens is either a result of external forces or owing to oneself. There are some things that happen due to external circumstances and others due to one's own actions. In control fallacies, there is an excessive tendency to lean towards one or the other.

A person suffering from control fallacies distorted thinking either thinks that everything happens either due to external circumstances or one's own actions. For instance, when we are unable to put in our best effort, we perceive this as a result of working with inefficient or incompetent people. Thus, something that is a result of our own actions is blamed on an external cause, which may be untrue.

On the hand, people who blame themselves or their actions will blame themselves for everything that happens to other people too.

The Shoulds

The shoulds refer to rules people hold about how things or people should ideally act or speak. When these are violated by others, they tend to get upset. Also, when they break their own shoulds, they are overcome with feelings of guilt and regret. For instance, if these people believe that spending money for pleasure is an irresponsible act, they will feel guilty even for buying themselves a cup of coffee. The 'shoulds' are often rigid, staunch and irrational.

Change Fallacy

This pattern of distorted thinking has people thinking that other folks should change according to what is convenient for them. This is closely interwoven into the belief that all our happiness is dependent on others. It is people's unwillingness to change that causes our unhappiness. This is a highly distorted view where people place their happiness and sorrow in the hands of others and expect them to change to make us happy.

What Are Core Beliefs?

Core beliefs are often on the basis of involuntary and intrusive thoughts running through the mind. Recognizing and challenging these core beliefs does not just help in shifting feelings but basically transforms an individual's entire approach to living. We often assume core beliefs to be true and allow them to grow unchallenged. By identifying precise automatic or involuntary thoughts, it is possible to unearth one's underlying beliefs that eventually shape one's feelings, actions, and personalities.

Core beliefs can originate from early childhood experiences, cultural influences or inherent personality. It can also combine all factors. They are difficult to detect and change because they have become an inherent part of our personality. So ingrained are these beliefs within the personality that it is tough to identify them as challenging or attribute them to a clear source. Notice if any of these characteristics can be traced to your childhood or environmental experiences.

Defective Feelings

These beliefs involve a general feeling of being flawed, incapable or not good enough for anything. There is a deep rooted inferiority complex that you will never be good enough for anyone or that people will discover that you are essentially a bad or incompetent person.

Abandonment Fear

People who have core beliefs deeply entrenched in abandonment will often feel like they'll be abandoned by people they get emotionally attached to. There is an inherent sense of insecurity of losing people, and ultimately being confined to a life filled with isolation and misery.

Strong Sense of Self-Entitlement

Entitlement is when you assume a false sense of importance that reflects a need to be awarded special treatment. People suffering from a core belief of entitlement make demands or do things that make them feel special or important regardless of how it impacts others.

Challenging Core Beliefs with CBT

Core beliefs are more challenging to tackle than disturbing/intrusive or automatic thoughts. They are deeply ingrained in a person's life because they are generally rooted since the individual's most formative, early years (childhood or adolescence).

For instance, if a child has constantly been told in childhood that he was born out of an unwanted pregnancy while the parents were still in college and that the child brought their lives to a standstill. The child grows up to believe he is worthless and unwanted, or that he doesn't deserve any love for being the cause of other people's trouble.

Our core beliefs are deeply embedded in the larger portion of the brain region which is known as schema (responsible for storing more general or prototype information or ideas that are utilized for arranging information in a logical manner to determine how we perceive something). When schema and matching beliefs are triggered, they process information in a subjective way. Information that is consistent with schema is pulled out, and that which isn't consistent with schema is shunned. This only ends up feeding the core beliefs even more.

CBT for modifying core beliefs starts with the client and therapist identifying these underlying beliefs. While some clients have a fairly clear awareness of their basic problem (inferiority complex as a result of being constantly admonished in childhood), others are clueless about more deeply rooted experiences.

One of the most widely used strategies for recognizing core beliefs is the Downward Arrow technique, originally introduced by Aron Beck, Rush Shaw, and Emery, and later expounded upon by Burns. Therapists ask continuous questions to understand the meaning of automatic or involuntary thoughts until they uncover a core belief. For instance, if a person suffers from social anxiety, they'll ask if she is afraid of being negatively judged by people. Or if she thinks she is not good enough, etc. until they arrive at a clear core belief.

A popular CBT strategy for altering core beliefs is to critically assess evidence in support of the long held belief and evidence in favor of a newer, more positive core belief. The goal (established at the onset) is to collect a large volume of evidence supporting the healthier, new belief. The therapist may use the cognitive restructuring techniques to challenge the long held core beliefs with evidence of more constructive beliefs.

Chapter Four:

Effective Self-Help Cognitive Behavioral Techniques

There are countless cognitive behavioral techniques that a therapist can come up with, or you can practice based on the unique conditions and magnitude of the issue. However, you don't always have to wait for a therapist to start CBT. There are innumerable small ways in which you can apply CBT techniques in your everyday life. You can also use a combination of your own strategies and those suggested by the therapist to create a more comprehensive treatment plan.

Here are some of the most workable self-help cognitive behavioral techniques that can be incorporated into your daily living.

Behavior Experiments

This is where you establish a goal and test different thoughts that trigger a specific unwanted behavior pattern. For instance, if you are suffering from binge eating, and are practicing CBT to treat overeating, you test different self-talk and thoughts that reduce the tendency to overeat. Does self-criticism following a binge eating session work better than being kind to yourself after over eating? Practice different behavior patterns to gauge what works best to stop you from over eating.

Try varied approaches on different occasions, while monitoring the result of each of your eating patterns. This will offer you an objective feedback on the effectiveness of each technique in controlling binge eating. This technique can help counteract or eliminate any misconceptions and offer you the best strategy for combating the condition. In the above example, you may realize that having a kind and motivating pep talk with yourself after a binge eating session can be more effective that self-criticism.

You can also say or write some affirmations that train your subconscious mind to believe in more positive thoughts, therefore directing your body towards more positive actions.

Positive Activity Scheduling

Positive activity or pleasant activity scheduling is especially helpful for those suffering from depression. It works like this (can be worked upon by your therapist in greater detail).

Count seven days from the day you begin, and schedule one positive/pleasant activity that you love doing for each day. It should be something that you truly enjoy, and that isn't harmful to you (so yes, no binge drinking sessions and junk food overload).

It could be a hobby you've long since given up or something that you just haven't had the time for of late. Read a novel, go fishing, take a cooking class, paint, have lunch at your favorite café – anything that you haven't done recently and which you truly cherish.

Another version of this technique is to do one thing (each day) that gives you a clear sense of accomplishment. Start with something small that takes less than 15 minutes of your day.

The advanced variation of this CBT strategy is to plan three positive activities each day – one for morning, another for noon and the third for evening. Indulging in activities that trigger feel-good emotions in everyday living helps reduce your negative thinking patterns, secretes more feel-good hormones in the brain and makes you less self-focused.

Situation Exposure

This is another excellent CBT technique that works well for anxiety and phobias. It consists of putting together a thematic list of things that you would normally escape or want to avoid. Thus, a person suffering from acute social anxiety may find the prospect of asking someone out on a date the scariest.

You make a list of things that you dread and rate them based on how stressed or anxious they make you feel on a scale of 1-10. Work your way from the least scary to the scariest. So, a person in the above example may find it least scary to ask a member of the opposite sex for directions. However, the scariest may be asking them out on a date.

Begin with the least scary situation and practice it multiple times until the anxiety experienced for it is reduced by half of what it was before you began the task. So if asking a member of the opposite sex for directions rated 4/10 on your anxiety meter, work until it is reduced to 2/10. Gradually work your way through the list with every item, and follow the same pattern.

Recording Thoughts

Thoughts records are created to evaluate points for and against a particular belief we hold. It is similar to an internal debate where we are challenging our negative/destructive thoughts with evidence to the contrary.

Take for example, you receive a negative feedback from your manager, and start believing that you aren't good for anything. Now, look for evidence that contradicts this negative belief. Think about all the times your manager offered you a positive feedback. Doesn't it outnumber the negative feedback? Think about all the instances where your coworkers asked you for guidance.

Would your manager waste time on you by giving you feedback if he/she didn't consider you good enough? Don't they want you to be the best, which is why they are offering scope for improvement? These are the kind of thought patterns that challenge your negative, self-critical thoughts.

Once you consider a more objective assessment of the situation with both for and against your belief, there is a higher chance of coming up with objective or balanced thoughts. The tendency to think in extremes gradually decreases, which leads to lower anxiety or depression over a period of time.

Recording our thoughts is helpful because it acts as a tangible proof of our unfounded thoughts and balanced thoughts. While writing your positive thoughts, your subconscious mind is internalizing them even more, thus leading to more positive behavior and actions.

Thought experiments like these are helpful for challenging self-critical beliefs on a rational plane, whereas more behavior oriented experiments are useful when it comes to challenging a gut feeling or emotional experiences, irrespective of more balanced evidence stating otherwise.

Imagery Exposure

Imagery exposure is particularly helpful when a single recent event has triggered strong emotional reactions leading to the condition. For instance, a person has been laid off by an organization where he devoted several years. In imagery exposure, he is asked to go through the entire situation that caused distress in detail and label his emotions objectively.

He'll start by remembering the tone of his manager's voice, the manager's cabin, and the manager's expressions – there is a lot of emphasis on sensory details or imagery. Next, he will label his thoughts objectively. In prolonged sessions, the individual keeps visualizing the pictures in detail till his distress/anxiety level reduces by about a half of what it was originally.

Cognitive Restructuring

As soon as one identifies a pattern of distorted perceptions about oneself or the world, it is easier to challenge those skewed ideas. You learn to assess objectively (during CBT sessions) how the belief took birth, why it is incorrect and how it can prevent you from leading a rewarding life. Thus, begins the process of challenging these beliefs.

For instance, you have always held the belief that those who have a successful and high-paying job are respectable folks. One fine day you're laid off from your top paying job, and you stop believing that you are worthy of respect. Thus, you begin to pity yourself and feel you aren't good enough.

Thus, you begin challenging your long held beliefs about what makes a person respectable. Being creative, resourceful and thinking out of the box can also make a person respectable, something you have plenty of opportunities to do now. This isn't something you may have considered earlier. When you challenge unreasonable thoughts that form your core, they can be turned into more objective beliefs and actions.

Play It Until the End

This CBT is helpful especially in cases of anxiety and phobia, where a person imagines the worst outcome of his fear. Thus, if a person suffers from social anxiety, he may imagine the worst case scenario of being ridiculed by people publically.

Playing the scenario in his mind allows him to learn that even in the worst possible case, things won't be as bad as he imagines them to be. It is a kind of experiment, which helps a person recognize that even if what he dreads comes true, it will be alright.

Deep Breathing

This is another relaxed deep breathing technique that isn't really CBT in the truest sense but can be used to supplement

CBT techniques in cases of anxiety (Obsessive Compulsive Disorder, intrusive thoughts, etc.).

Focusing attention on your breath and bringing more regularity/control in breathing helps you manage your emotions and actions more effectively. It is said to lead to a more balanced state of mind. There are multiple ways to relax and bring greater regularity to the breathing pattern.

Some ways include guided and uninstructed visual imagery (visualization meditation) through YouTube videos and other audio recordings to calm the breath and let people approach their challenges with a more objective perspective, thus creating more effective thinking and rational behavior.

The best part is it can be used in treating mental conditions such as panic, OCD, phobias, other types of anxiety, and even depression. You don't need a therapist to practice deep, relaxed breathing.

Journaling

This technique is closely incorporated into CBT in many cases as a means of uncovering our innermost or underlying emotions. It is a data gathering exercise for our emotions, thoughts, actions, and moods. It can help identify thought patterns, causal links between thoughts/feeling and actions, and the intensity of our thoughts. It helps us recognize emotional triggers, and our spontaneous response to it, among several other things.

Journaling also acts as a sort of catharsis, especially in cases of depression, where writing our innermost feelings makes us feel slightly relieved. When we describe our feelings in detail, it is easy to change them or deal with them.

5 CBT Techniques for Fighting Depression

Depending on the gravity of the conditions and several other factors, CBT for depression typically lasts for six weeks. The therapist may work with you closely to counteract negative or depressive thinking patterns. He/she will also guide you to continue practicing the techniques by yourself. Here are some of the most popular CBT techniques that you and your therapist can work on to reduce symptoms of chronic depression.

Identifying the Issue and Brainstorm

One of the best ways to identify the root cause of your condition is to write down your innermost feelings or to talk freely with your therapist. What triggers a particular behavior pattern? Why do you feel the way you do? Write down everything exactly the way you feel it.

One of the most prevalent and common themes running across most cases of depression is a feeling of complete hopelessness. There's an underlying belief that the situation will never improve. Sit with your therapist and make a list of everything that can be done to challenge the feeling of hopelessness.

For example, a person who is fighting loneliness post-divorce can try to join a local dating club for singles or be a part of a traveling club for singles. They could sign up with online dating sites and meet people who are in a similar situation or have experienced the same heartbreak. These folks can also enjoy a club or society based on their interests like reading, knitting or cooking club. The idea is to battle loneliness by meeting like-minded people and doing something that makes them happy.

Write Positive Statements

Write positive affirmations or self-statements to challenge negative ones taking shape in your mind. If you and the therapist have successfully identified the issue, use all the positive statements and thoughts to replace negative or depressive feelings. Counteracting or replacing negative thoughts with positive ones is the key here.

Keep repeating the self-statements to yourself. When you write them or speak them in a loop, a tiny niggling negative voice will try to snuff it out. However, gradually, you'll learn to kill the negative thoughts and help your positive ones grow even stronger. The negative voices will slowly lose energy and die a natural death if they aren't fed over a period of time.

Therapists often suggest that the self-statements or positive statements should not be too far off from the original negative thought. This means you don't think you are absolutely bad at something, rather, you simply think that though you aren't good at something, you will get better at it with practice. It's like balancing or neutralizing negative thoughts to make them less illogical and irrational.

Similarly, when you are depressed, you don't emphasize on, "I am terribly depressed now" or "I am feeling so delighted now", you simply balance it out with "sometimes you feel better, while other times you feel low, my life too has the highs and lows experienced by everyone else." This makes it a more digestible statement than "Oh! I am so bright, chirpy and happy all the time", which appears more forced and unreal.

The whole idea is that it's fine to say that you are feeling better than you actually are while keeping it well within check to save the mind from disappointment.

You may feel stuck in routine or rut while repeating the same self-statements. It's alright to vary them, create them in other languages, rephrase them or make them more fun. For example, you may want to say, "I am enjoying an incredibly "up" day today" instead of "I am feeling good today or having a lovely day today."

Find Opportunities for Triggering Positive Thoughts

Identify opportunities that trigger positive thoughts. For instance, you are the kind of person who enters a room and says, "Oh that wall color is so depressing," train your brain to identify three positive elements in the room. Consciously start looking for positive things wherever you go. Set a positive thought reminder on your phone where you remind yourself to reframe negative thoughts into positive ones.

Another neat tip is to find a positive thought buddy. If someone else is caught in a similar negative thinking pattern situation, buddy up with him/her and work together on the technique. You both can share your positive thoughts/experiences through the day with greater enthusiasm and motivation.

Visualize the Best of Each Day

End each day by visualizing the best things that happened during the day. You can close your eyes and visualize them as they happened or record them in a journal. Many therapists suggest making a gratitude list, which is writing down everything that you are thankful for in your life. Simply go over the best things that happened during the change and gradually witness how your thought perception changes its negative and depressive frequency.

At the end of each day, make a list of things you are thankful for and try not to repeat the same blessings. Include everything from your vision to the air around you to a roof over your head to just about every blessing you are thankful for. When you start writing everything that is good about your life, your subconscious mind automatically latches on to those positive feelings and directs your thoughts, feelings, and actions to be more positive.

Writing your blessings or positive feelings at the end of each day creates a brain pathway for more positive feelings, where you wake up with thoughts like, "what a wonderful day it is going to be" over "ugh, just another terrible workday."

Learn To Embrace Disappointments

Disappointments and failures are integral to one's existence, and your reaction to them can dramatically affect how you overcome them and move ahead. Our feelings are largely determined by our ability to cope with challenging situations in life. For instance, someone who has just been laid off will think, "What's the point of working hard, developing new skills and taking courses?"

However, a more positive approach during this adversity is to upgrade one's skill, go back to college or take a course that adds to your profile. Being laid off was a business decision directed by market forces which were beyond your control.

However, doing positive or constructive things with the time you've earned is totally in your control.

There are disappointing situations or challenges that are beyond our realm of control; however how we react to them is absolutely in our control. Overlook things that are out of your control (external circumstances), and focus on things that are within your control (your reaction).

Chronicle your feelings in a journal if that helps. Write what happened, what you ended up learning from the entire experience, how you can prevent it from happening next time (if it's within your control) and what you are going to do now.

Consciously watch out for negative thoughts and blank them out slowly. This will help you feel even better about things coming up in future. The acceptance of disappointments technique saves you from playing the victim of circumstance and instead lets you proactively take the onus of your life in a more positive direction.

4 CBT Techniques for Anxiety

As seen in the previous chapter, the symptoms of anxiety vary from the symptoms of depression, which means behavioral therapy can be slightly different for both. In depression, there is an undercurrent of hopelessness and despair, while in anxiety the goal is to contain an underlying fear or worry.

Act Normal

Anxiety isn't an ailment, it is more a condition related to survival response. Sometimes even if the response feels involuntarily helpful in ensuring survival, it is a hindrance because it takes on extreme proportions.

For instance, you have a guard dog at home watching out for the safety and security of your home. The pizza delivery man walks in one day, and the dog bites him. Now, the dog bit the man to ensure your safety but ended up doing more harm even with the best of intentions.

Your anxiety is pretty similar. When you sense a threat, your mind and body automatically react to it, though the reaction is based more on perceived threat than an actual threat. This can be slowly decreased by training the brain to be pickier when it comes to protecting you. It's like giving out a subtle message that "your help is not needed" to the brain. Let the brain look out for signals when it comes to determining what is normal and what isn't.

Start doing the following things when you feel the need to run or withdraw due to a perceived threat – talk calmly, smile, breathe deeply and keep a relaxed body posture.

When people suffering from anxiety adopt one or all of these techniques, they modify the feedback given to their anxiety response system or the nervous system. They send a clear feedback that if the perceived fear was real; the body wouldn't be breathing, talking or smiling normally. The very fact that the body is able to do these things normally means that there is no real threat.

A lot of people are advised to chew gum when they begin experiencing anxiety. This is because chewing gum produces saliva, and sets the body up for normal eating and chewing functions. Therefore, the fear response system gets a message that if the threat was indeed real, the body wouldn't be able to function in a normal manner producing saliva for eating.

Do we ever eat in life threatening situations? It is only during comfortable situations that our body can perform normal functions. This is why therapists urge clients to do normal tasks and act normal when they feel stressed or anxious.

It gradually switches off the anxiety response mode, which leads to a huge confidence boost for patients suffering from anxiety. Bringing a thought or action of normalcy in an otherwise perceived catastrophic situation helps alleviate the symptoms of anxiety.

Chase Rational Conclusions

When people feel anxious about a particular thing, they suffer from acute fear of the consequences. For instance, if they suffer from social anxiety, they may fear the consequences of attending a party or meeting new folks. Run over all the possible consequences in your mind.

People may not like you, you will be upset, you will end up feeling isolated, and you will feel you aren't worthy of being liked. Now that you've imagined the worst, how do you plan to deal with it? You can focus on people who like you to prove your assumptions about people not liking you wrong.

When people are insecure about their relationships, have them expand on what it is that they fear the most. Will the relationship break? That isn't as big a catastrophe as we imagine it to be. It may be a step in the right direction towards a better relationship. The realization that the individual can survive and thrive despite undergoing what he/she perceives to be a threat to their survival chokes insecurity or worry.

Powerful feelings mold thoughts, which means when we lift our feelings, the thoughts invariably change their rhythm leading to a calmer emotional state. Reframing feelings are useful because it helps people realize that feeling positive by anticipating the worst can change our fundamental thoughts about the anxiety causing object or situation.

What we are doing is simply altering the behavioral feedback being sent to the nervous system that there's no emergency fear situation and that anything that happens is absolutely in control, which makes the person feel more confident, assured and balanced.

While taking the path of rational conclusions, we tell the brain it is possible to survive or even thrive in the worst situation.

Identify Rumination Patterns

Rumination is a pattern where a person is repeatedly held hostage to worry or nervousness. They keep going over the negative consequences of the problem, which decreases their rational or problem-solving abilities. When you're ruminating, it's best to find a solution to the issue without slipping into rumination.

Use a smart phone to record your rumination patterns. When you are ruminating, what do you most likely think about? Are you completely lost thinking about the consequences of your fear? Do you think about the past or future? Do you feel an avalanche of negative emotions? These can be indicators that you're ruminating.

Being aware of the fact that you're ruminating is the key to stopping your rumination patterns. Simply record the action taken for each instance of rumination at the end of the day. Calculate the ratio of rumination and action taken to resolve the issue at the end of each week.

The best way to deal with ruminating thoughts is to recognize or identify them as ruminations and accept that they may not always be accurate. Let the thoughts run their time since trying to forcefully block them will only increase their intensity, making them more intrusive and distressing.

Have a plan in place before you begin ruminating about how you plan to tackle it. It can be the above-mentioned technique of removing your phone and recording the rumination pattern. Come up with rational, logical and realistic evidence that suggests that the thing/situation you are ruminating about is unfounded. Gradually, shift focus to finding solutions for the rumination pattern.

Avoiding a Relapse

Dealing with anxiety is pretty much like working out in a gym to keep in top shape. If you don't make it a consistent, daily routine, you won't accomplish the desired results. Many times, people suffering from anxiety or even depression do not practice cognitive behavioral therapy regularly, and slip into earlier habits, thus leading to a relapse. It is especially more marked in times of pain, a sudden unfortunate event or fatigue.

Keep practicing your cognitive behavioral therapies regularly. To make it even simpler, break your goals into weekly tasks. Try and come up with a schedule of your action plan for the week. Eliminate all warning signs or triggers from your everyday living to make yourself less vulnerable to anxiety. For instance, if arguing with a loved one makes you slip into unhappiness, which eventually leads to anxiety, try and eliminate situations causing those arguments.

Being aware of your red flags helps you nip them in the bud before they rear their ugly head. Also, have an action plan to cope with these feelings rather than slipping back into anxiety. The action plan can be practicing calm breathing or converting negative thoughts into more positive or balanced thoughts.

Overcoming anxiety, depression or any mental condition is a perpetual work in progress. One of the best ways to avoid slipping back into it is to keep working with new and challenging situations, where you are continuously coming up with different ways to challenge an unreasonable thought process or behavior.

When you slip into a relapse (which isn't unnatural), quickly identify what caused it. Next time, have a clear plan to cope with the cause.

Your thoughts about the relapse will largely determine the success or failure of overcoming the condition. If you consider all the hard work a waste, and that there is just no hope, you'll stop putting the effort and slip deeper into relapse mode.

Instead, try to think of how you've come a long way and how it is next to impossible to simply unlearn everything about overcoming anxiety. You've learned to handle it, and it's just about getting back to track. Think about this. Do you forget how to drive once you learn it? Of course, the skills may get slightly rusty if you don't practice for long. However, you aren't going to forget driving.

Relapses are a given, and they can be challenged. Don't brand yourself a loser or failure simply because you relapsed. Treat yourself with gentleness and kindness, and realize that this is something you can overcome.

Conclusion

Thank you for choosing "Cognitive Behavioral Therapy: Master Your Brain, Depression And Anxiety".

I hope you enjoyed reading it and were able to learn more about Cognitive Behavioral Techniques and how they can be used to treat various psychological conditions such as depression and anxiety. I also hope it offered you plenty of actionable ideas, practical tips, and wisdom nuggets to challenge negative/self-destructive mental conditions.

Keep in mind that the treatment of any mental condition is a constant work in progress. You have to be consistent and determined while practicing these techniques and continue (even when you feel better) in order to experience stellar results.

The next step is to go out there and use all the proven strategies mentioned in the book. Treating your condition will certainly not be an overnight process. Apply the techniques mentioned in the book in your daily life consistently and slowly, but surely, you'll witness positive results.

You'll slowly transform from an unsure person struggling with your emotions as well as other people's emotions to an emotionally evolved and socially adjusted individual, who will enjoy better interpersonal relationships and lead a more fulfilling life.

Emotional Intelligence

Master The Strategies

To Improve Your Emotional Intelligence,

Build Self-Confidence, And Find Long Lasting Success

Written by

George Muntau

Introduction

Congratulations on purchasing "Emotional Intelligence: Master The Strategies To Improve Your Emotional Intelligence, Build Self-Confidence, And Find Long Lasting Success", thank you for doing so. The world is evolving on how to handle your emotions and this book is your first step in knowing how to handle your emotions.

The first step that you have taken is important in helping you master your emotions. This book will have ways in which you can implement immediately. Filing away what you will learn from this book for the future, will be a sure way of you knowing how to combat situations that seem to trigger your strongest emotions.

The following chapters will discuss what emotional intelligence (EQ or EI) looks like and how to identify if you have any. This means you will learn the different emotional intelligence skills that are there and how they affect your life on a daily basis and if you can identify any of the skills mentioned.

After learning what EQ looks like, you will learn the actions that you can take to help you identify the emotional intelligence skills you are low at. The Emotional Intelligence Appraisal test is a sure way of grading yourself. There are strategies that come into play for you to understand the skills better and improve what you already have.

With all these knowledge, you will get to know what discoveries have been made since EQ was discovered and how it plays an important role in the current business world, by comparing America and China.

There are plenty of books on the market that cover this topic, thank you for selecting this one! Plenty of effort was put in place to make sure it had useful information, enjoy!

Chapter 1

What Emotional Intelligence Looks Like

Before you even get to know what emotional intelligence looks like, it is important to understand what emotional intelligence is. There are various definitions of emotional intelligence (EQ or EI), like:

- The ability to recognize your own emotions and those of others, for managing feelings well in our relationships, ourselves and for motivating ourselves.

- It is the capacity to understand, use, identify and manage your own emotions in positive ways to empathize with others, communicate effectively, defuse conflict, relieve stress and overcome challenges.

- The capacity to comprehend and recognize what others are going through emotionally.

There are two kinds of intelligence – emotional and intellectual - which also express different parts of the brain's activity.

179

Intellectual Intelligence - is based on the workings of the neocortex, which is the more recently evolved layer found at the top of the brain.

Emotional Intelligence - found in the more ancient sub cortex of the brain; its centers are lower in the brain. Emotional intelligence works hand in hand with these emotional centers and the intellectual centers.

Many people tend to have a rough time connecting with the current modern society we live in and this can be with others and also ourselves. Emotional intelligence plays a key role in being able to connect with others and adapt to the society. Relationship successes, personal and professional goals all depend on our emotional intelligence (EQ) as well our intellectual intelligence (IQ).

In general, most people who are book smart tend to have a low EQ or lack emotional intelligence and they always work for people who are not as smart as they are but have an excellent emotional intelligence skill. Emotional intelligence is learned, not acquired and can take place at any moment of our lives. It is something that we all can have.

It is necessary to have emotional intelligence, as it turns our intentions into actions, we get to connect in a nurturing and productive manner with others inclusive of making informed decisions.

Howard Gardner, a Harvard psychologist, proposed in 1983 a widely regarded model of "multiple intelligence". He listed seven kinds of intelligence that included two "personal" varieties; social adeptness and knowing one's inner world. Other theories were proposed by two scientists in 1990, Peter Salovey at Yale and John Mayer who is at the University of New Hampshire. The two defined emotional intelligence as being able to monitor your own as well as others' emotions and use feelings to guide your thoughts and impulses.

Learning about emotional intelligence and applying it are two different things. You may know what you should do but that does not mean that you will do it. Stress, despair, anger, and disliking someone can play a major role in how you react to a situation. You need to learn to be emotionally conscious by learning how to stand up when under pressure and ways to overcome stress.

There are four attributes to emotional intelligence:

1. Relationship management which is how you develop and maintain good relationships, influence and inspire others, manage conflict and communicate clearly.

2. Self-awareness helps you recognize your own emotions and how they affect your behavior and thought. Getting to know our weaknesses and strengths and having self-confidence.

3. Social awareness – understanding others' needs, concerns and emotions, feeling comfortable in a social setting and recognizing power dynamics in a group setting or organization.

4. Self-management which helps you to control impulsive behaviors and feelings. Follow through with your commitments, adapt to changing environments and also ways in which you can manage your emotions in a healthy manner.

They can further be subdivided into two primary competencies:

Personal Competence - It is the capacity to be aware of your emotions and be able to manage your tendencies and behavior. It is made up of self-awareness and self-management skills. They are more about you as an individual than your interaction with other people.

Social Competence - This is the capacity to comprehend other people's behaviors, needs, moods, and motives so that you can improve the quality of your relationships. It is comprised of social awareness and relationship management skills.

All these attributes play a key role in knowing what emotional intelligence looks like. Here, we are going to look at each attribute and how they are in action.

1. Self-awareness

Your capacity to accurately understand your emotions in the moment and comprehend your tendencies across situations is the definition of self-awareness.

For you to actually know what your emotions are like and how you react to situations is by spending a lot of time thinking through it, figuring out where they emanate from and why they are present. Our emotions originate from somewhere; some come from life experiences and past situations that are somewhat similar.

Understanding what makes you think in a straightforward and honest way is self-awareness, not your deep dark conscious or unconscious motives. Thinking about it helps you to improve on it even though most of the times we tend to focus on what we did wrong.

When you are self-aware, you are not afraid of your emotional mistakes. You get to know what you should do differently and the information that you need to understand will flow as life goes on. Having self-awareness skill makes it easier for you to use the other emotional intelligence skills.

Having self-awareness skills makes you:

- Open, authentic, and capable of handling difficult situations with people by keeping the conversation appropriate and watching your tone.

When you lack self-awareness, most people may refer to you as:

- Defensive, aggressive, and demanding even though you don't mean to be.

You can come off being too focused on an outcome missing the process to get to the end especially when working with a group. You can talk over someone when you are excited, not letting them have a chance to talk.

2. Self-management

This is the definition of whatever occurs when you act or don't act and is dependent on your self-awareness. It is how you direct your behavior positively depending on your emotions. Self-management is more than just avoiding explosive situations; it is how you manage your tendencies over time and how you apply your skill in various situations.

Identifying your self-control comes from putting momentary needs on hold and pursuing larger and more important goals. It is difficult to do so and you'll be tested over and over on your self-management. Putting your needs on hold and managing your tendencies is a sure way of succeeding in whatever you are doing.

Self-management can be spotted by others when they say you:

- Communicate properly, have patience and understanding when dealing with people in difficult situations.

- You can handle stressful situations and confrontations very well.

Lacking self-management makes you come off as:

- Emotional, when circumstances are out of your control and you mainly let your emotions rule your behavior.

- You have verbal outbursts when stressed.

- Being too honest that is demoralizing someone.

- You tend to be proactive instead of reactive as you tell others of your issues but do not take a time to listen to theirs.

3. Social Awareness

This is the capacity to pick up on other peoples' emotions and understand what is really happening in their lives. It is more of perceiving what others are feeling and thinking, even if you do not reciprocate the same.

The most important aspects of social awareness are listening and observing. This is possible by not doing what we like to do but paying attention to what is going on around us. Try not to think of your next point, stop talking and anticipate what the person talking is going to say next.

Try and be an anthropologist, they tend to live watching others in their natural state without letting their thoughts and feelings come into play. Watch others as you interact with them as this will give you an inkling of whatever they are feeling and thinking.

Being an astute part of the interaction while still paying attention to the other person's emotions is what social awareness is all about.

Social awareness looks like this when you have it:

- You are able to build relationships with almost anyone and can read and adjust different situations with other people's emotions.

- You acknowledge other people's emotions when communicating difficult news.

- You have an interest in what other people are saying and doing and you offer insight based on what they have said to you.

- Lack of social awareness can be seen in the following ways:

- You lack patience when dealing with people.

- You do not allow people to feel good about their ideas even if you have a better idea.

- You do socialize with others as you are focused on work and might come off as not interested in what is going on in other people's lives.

4. Relationship Management

This is the capacity to understand one's emotions and those of others in order to explore through interactions successfully. The bond formed by interacting with people over time. Strengthened relationships are as a result of how you treat people; understand them and the history you share with them.

When stressed, how you interact with people is challenged. At work, conflicts tend to fester when people refuse to address the obvious challenge in the room. Taking out your anger on people is common especially at work, because of suppressed anger or frustration. Relationship management gives you the skills required to handle such situations and have better interactions with people.

Relationship management looks like this:

- Having the ability to read other people's emotions and using that to create a safe environment for you to carry out a discussion.

- You are sensitive to other people and make situations better.

- You are an empathetic listener and have patience.

- When not pleased with results obtained, you express your opinions with thoughtful insight without shouting or anger.

- You know when to give praise and encouragement.

Lack of relationship management looks like this:

- You cannot form relations with someone if they do not share your ideas.

- You minimize the opinions or point of view of others.

- When working with subordinates, you come off blunt and not empathetic.

- You are judgmental and you make hurtful remarks about your fellow workmates.

Chapter 2

Action Plan to Increase Your EQ

Once you understand that EQ is important, there are areas in which you might be low in and need to increase your EQ levels. You might want to be a better manager and deal with conflicts at work in a much professional way than you are handling it right now or you are doing a poor job at empathizing with your friends and their situations. All these situations can be solved through improving your emotional intelligence.

At work places, according to Talent Smart ™, over 90% of high performers have a high EQ, while 80% of low performers have low EQ. To maintain, enhance, develop, and form close relationships, emotional intelligence is a crucial element. The main disparity between IQ and EQ is that IQ will not change significantly for a lifetime whereas your EQ will evolve and increase depending on one's yearning to grow and learn.

Here are some ways in which you can enhance your emotional intelligence.

1. Stay Calm and Regulate Stress.

In life, we experience certain levels of stress. The way we manage that stress is the difference between being poised versus being frazzled and being reactive versus being assertive.

It is important to keep your cool when under pressure as this will help you control your actions and the words you speak. Here are some ways of doing so:

- At some point, if you feel discouraged, depressed, or fearful, try intense aerobic exercises. Make sure you energize yourself because the way you use your body will affect the way you feel. Do not have caffeinated beverages as they stimulate nervousness. The vitality of your body can increase your confidence.

- Put cool water on your visage and get some fresh air when you feel anxious and nervous. Cool temperatures help to reduce your anxiety levels.

2. The Ability to Reduce Negative Emotions

The most important aspect of EQ is being able to control your negative emotions. This is to avoid being overwhelmed by negative emotions that can affect your judgment. When you understand the way you digest a situation, you will eventually change the way you feel about it.

For instance:

- To reduce your fear of rejection, in important situations, provide yourself with multiple options in case anything happens, there will be alternatives to help you move forward. The saying of don't put all your eggs in one basket apply here. Identify a viable Plan B to maybe D should Plan A not work out.

This can be used when applying for jobs; instead of applying for one job apply for three jobs. If one does not pan out, you have two jobs that you are well qualified for. This reduces the chance of you feeling devastated.

- When you do not like someone, do not jump to negative conclusions immediately. Instead, devise different ways of assessing the person before having a reaction. When you do not personalize another person's behavior, you then view their actions more open-mindedly. It is all about them, not you or us.

Apply this when dealing with a friend, who might be ignoring you, consider the option of them being busy. Increase your perspective to reduce the chances of misunderstanding situations or people.

3. Being Able to Bounce Back from Adversity

What can make a difference between victory and defeat, hope and despair and optimism and frustration is how we choose to act, think, and feel in relation to the challenges that we face in our day-to-day lives. We need to ask ourselves, "What is most important now?" "How should I learn from this encounter?" and "What is the lesson here?" after every challenging situation that we encounter.

In the case of Abraham Lincoln, he failed several times and had a nervous breakdown, but he did not give up. He went through all these trials and tribulations but eventually became the 16th United States president.

To receive better quality answers, we need to ask better quality questions. Constructive questions based on priorities and learning will help one gain proper perspective to handle the situation at hand.

Michael Jordan says with the 9000 shots in his career, losing 300 games with 26 of those being trusted to make the winning shot but he missed. Failing over and over and over again is what make him succeed.

4. Expressing Difficult Emotions and Being Assertive

It is important to set boundaries in some situations in our lives so that people know where we stand. It can be to disagree, saying 'no' without feeling guilty afterward, protecting oneself from harm and duress, or getting what one paid for.

Using the XYZ technique is one method you can use to express difficult emotions. I feel X when you do Y in situation Z

For instance:

"I feel uncomfortable when you expect me to help you all the time with your duties when I have duties of my own."

"I feel disappointed when you do not follow through with the plans you told me you would."

To avoid sentences that make you sound judgmental or accusatory, do not start a sentence with "you are...," "you need to...," or "you should...". The listener is always on the defense after such statements, and they are likely not to open up and say what they want to.

To quote Harriet Lerner "being who we are requires that we can talk openly about things that are important to us, that we take a clear position on where we stand on important emotional issues, and that we clarify the limits of what is acceptable and tolerable to us in a relationship".

5. Being Able to Express Intimate Emotions in Close and Personal Relationships

Maintaining close personal relationships requires both parties involved to express their emotions effectively. This means sharing those emotions in a manner that is constructive and nurturing and also being able to have an affirmative response when it is the other way around.

"Bidding" is a method of an affirmative relation between two people who desire to have an intimate relationship. This term is the definitive expression of deep emotions, according to psychologist Dr. John Gottman.

An example can be through:

- Body language bidding is through smiling, arm around shoulder, positive eye contact.

- Verbal bidding such as "I'm sorry.", "I love you.", "How are you doing?", or "I look forward to spending time together."

- Behavioral bidding like a thoughtful gift, offering food and beverage.

Research done by Dr. Gottman revealed that close, healthy relationships bid with each other in small and large ways many times in a day. Gestures and words can be a million variations, which in essence say, "I care about you," and "you are very important in my life." Maintaining and developing close personal relationships require consistent and constant bidding.

6. Being Proactive and not Reactive when Facing a Difficult Person.

It is common to have a difficult or unreasonable person, be it at home or at work, and they can affect your day immensely and quite easily. There are some ways of staying proactive in such situations:

Assert and identify consequences — This is very vital when you are trying to stand down an unreasonable person. When you devise well-articulated consequences, the difficult person is likely to pause and they will shift from violence to respect for you.

Take a deep breath and count slowly backward to ten — When you feel upset or angry with someone, this will help you not to say something that you might regret later. You would have come up with a better response to the issue at hand by the time you count to ten. This reduces the chances of complicating the situation you are facing. In case you are still angry after mentally counting to ten, remove yourself from the situation, and return after you have calmed down.

For just a moment, place yourself in the difficult one's shoes — This is by considering the person one is dealing with and being able to know or see why they are behaving the way they do. Empathetic statements like "It must not be easy…"

"My boss is extremely demanding. It must not be easy to have such demands placed on her performance by the management..."

These do not excuse one's behavior but makes us reasonable and considerate when dealing with a difficult individual. Have an omnipresent view of the way you view a situation and be more objective, then devise better ways of dealing with it.

You can also come up with an Emotional Intelligence Action Plan to help guide you through the process:

1. **Do an Emotional Intelligence Appraisal test-** This will help you know which EQ skill you need to improve on.

2. **Work through one EQ skill after another** – After you receive the results of the Appraisal test, work through one skill at a time. However, it is recommended that you don't start with relationship management if you scored below 75% all through in all four EQ skills.

3. **Pick three strategies to use for your chosen skill** – The feedback from the Appraisal test will have strategies. Choose what to use for the selected skill.

4. **Get an EQ mentor** – Find someone who has mastered the skill you have chosen and ask if they are willing to help you out.

5. **As you apply your chosen strategies, keep in mind;**

    a) **Don't expect perfection, instead, expect success** – Continue to hold yourself back when emotions get out of control.

    b) **Practice, practice and more practice** – Practice your strategies as often as you can, with different people in different settings.

    c) **Be patient** – It will take time to notice a lasting change. For some people, it takes three to six months. Take your time and do not give up.

6. **Do measure your progress** – When you have noted that sufficient progress has been made on your chosen skill, do the Appraisal test a second time then complete the action plan's part two.

Chapter 3

Understanding Your EQ

It is well known that the smartest people around are never the best when it comes to being social or having relationships. You most probably have associated yourself with people who are socially inept and cannot hold a conversation with you for more than five minutes without going back to their phones to read their fanfiction, or sat down with people who cannot express their views in an empathetic manner while taking care not to step on anyone's emotions. But in both cases, these people turn out to be the best at studies or analytical problem-solving and are often seen at the top of the class.

Intellectual Quotient (IQ) is definitely not the only key to a successful life. It is quite possible to get into college with a high IQ but an Emotional Quotient (EQ) will help you when it comes to exam anxiety issues.

In 1990 psychologists Salovey and Mayer theorized when they were doing a study to explore the significance of emotional intelligence and develop valid measures. In the study, they found that there are four fundamental aspects to emotional intelligence. These are outlined as:

1. Recognizing emotions

2. Understanding emotions

3. Regulating emotions

4. Using your emotions

These four were defined as 'forms of social intelligence involving one's ability to monitor their own and other people's emotions, to differentiate them, and later use what you have garnered to guide your way of thinking and action.'

Develop your own EQ to help you understand the evolution of the social intelligence concept. You are likely to increase your professionalism at work and also improve how you interact with your family, coworkers, and everyone in your environment.

The four fundamental aspects of EQ and the studies done in psychological science bring to light the necessity of calming one's ego to bring out the best of themselves in any situation at any given time.

Success in life depends on the key balance, a Zen life within the world of extremities of social skills and intelligence in order to survive.

For a manager, it is important for you to know that in order to understand your subordinates and achieve business and personal objectives, you need to know who they really are. You need to grasp what emotional intelligence is and how you can make use of it when dealing with your employees, senior managers, suppliers and disgruntled customers.

Knowing your EI is one fundamental requirement in life. This understanding will help you navigate through any social setting, people who push your buttons and can help you deal with issues or situations that bring the worst in people.

The same way having a high IQ is important or required when applying for some jobs, having a great understanding of your EQ is also a requirement nowadays. Success is dependent on your ability to get along with everyone be it your subordinates and colleagues, teachers and students or the cashier at the local store. It also depends on your persistence in difficult situations.

With the four elements of emotional intelligence discussed in the previous chapter, the four elements work hand in hand to form a person who can survive through the most trying situations. It has been noted that you do not only need to have demonstrated your expertise and training at work, it is also required of you to show that you are able to handle yourself and others too, below or above you.

Developing your own EQ

Emotional intelligence has evolved over time and thus what you have acquired, needs to be applied in the environment you are working in. The importance of an individual's emotional intelligence has been noted as an important factor when you want to succeed in the working environment.

Consortium for Research on Emotional Intelligence (EQ or EI) in Organizations conducted a study to show the importance of EQ at work.

Study 1 — An analysis of over 300 top level executives from different global companies showed that there were six distinguishable emotional competencies:

- Team leadership

- Leadership

- Organizational awareness

- Self-confidence

- Influence and

- Achievement Drive

Study 2 – At L'Oreal, sales agents were selected by the analogy of either emotional competence or the company's previous methods. This research detailed that:

- Sales people chosen on the basis of emotional capability had 63% fewer turnovers during the first year than those selected through the company's methods.

- Sales people chosen through the emotional capability sold $91,370 more than the other sales people.

Study 3 – Experienced partners were assessed on the EI capabilities as well as the other partners and it was found that:

- Partners who scored above average on nine or more of the 20 capacities, delivered $1.2 million more returns than the other partners.

Study 4 – The output of "top performers" in jobs of medium complicacy, like clerks and mechanics, and the most complicated jobs such as account managers found that:

- Top performers in intricate jobs were 127% more accomplished than an average performer, while
- Top performers in mid-level complexity jobs were 12 times more accomplished than those at the bottom and 85% more accomplished than an average performer.

Study 5 – A national insurance company did a study on policy premiums sold. It was discovered that:

- Insurance agents that were very strong in a bare minimum of 5 out of 8 key emotional capacities sold policies worth more than $100,000.
- Those agents weak in emotional capacities sold policies below $60,000.

As shown in the studies above, having a high or above average emotional competence is what separates you from the rest of the crowd. You are likely to sell more, garner more clients and make your subordinates, colleagues or seniors respect you more because you are an easy person to work with.

Personal and Social Competencies

In order to get the hang of how your emotional intelligence skills are, there are two distinct competencies of your EQ:

i. Personal competencies that are made up of self-awareness and self-management.

ii. Social competencies comprise of social awareness and relationship management.

It is important to improve your competencies. Further, in the book, there are strategies discussed to help you achieve that, but first get to know which level you are in each of the competencies.

i. Personal Competency

Your level of this competency is only half of how you can develop your EQ further.

Self-awareness represents your foundation of EQ. If you lack this skill; you cannot move on to the other EQ competencies. Being aware of and understanding your own emotions is what you need to do first and foremost.

Self-management involves using the knowledge that you have about your emotions to manage those emotions as well as motivate yourself. Control your emotions and they are likely not to get the best of you in any situation.

We all don't always acknowledge that we have certain negative emotions, but the only way to overcome this is by having an awareness of what triggers these negative emotions. To find out if you have a high level of self-awareness skill, you will:

- Find out how your feelings affect your performance at work.
- Have an awareness of your life values and goals.

- Find new habits that will help reduce the impact your emotions are going to have in a situation.

- You will understand what emotions you are experiencing and why.

- Identify and acknowledge the links that are there between what you think, do and say and your feelings.

If you can identify which emotions make you react a certain way on particular scenarios, you will be able to properly assess yourself.

People with high level of self-confidence behave and communicate in a manner that shows that they:

- Are self-assured.

- Control the direction their lives take.

- Have certainty on their abilities.

- Aren't afraid to express an unpopular opinion, if it is what they believe.

- Make quick decisions under stressful situations.

For you to understand how self-management can have a positive impact in your life, you need to have the following attributes:

a) Conscientiousness – You are thorough, careful and have the desire to perform a task properly. You also tend to meet commitments and keep promises; organized in your work and also hold yourself accountable for your actions.

b) Adaptability – You can change something or yourself to fit circumstances you are facing. You are flexible to how you see events.

c) Initiative – You can come up with problem-solving resolutions and also take preventive measures to avoid situations from occurring. You generate new ideas; take a new or fresh perspective and risk in how you think.

d) Achievement Orientation – Make use of your time efficiently, gather information from others on how to get a job done and have a certain standard for excellence that you always work towards.

e) Trustworthiness – Your word is everything. You take a stand on topics that are unpopular and also stand with tough decisions if they need to be made.

f) Self-control

ii. Social Competence

Being socially aware of your surrounding and other people's emotions is important especially if you want to make them comfortable in your presence.

You need to have:

- *Empathy* – Comprehend other people's feelings. You have got to show your appreciation for their views and opinions; understand where emotional boundaries begin and end; listen actively to what they are saying and what they are expressing.

- *Service Orientation* – You assist other people's personal development by identifying situations that they can improve their productivity and ask questions carefully that can identify issues that are affecting someone's performance

- *Organizational Awareness* – You can read current emotions in groups. This helps when dealing with clients so that you can act on what the client's best interest is; the rationale behind the organization's structure and finally you understand how things are done — formally and informally— in the organization.

Relationship management competencies consist of:

✓ Conflict management which aids in recognizing, preventing and managing conflicts leading to a positive resolution. You are open-minded and willing to accept different perspectives and can read any underlying emotions that are present in a group.

✓ Building bonds with a large number of people and you are able to keep them informed on what is going on everywhere. These can be colleagues, professionals, friends, mentors and the everyday person you meet, like the barista, lunch lady or the bus driver too.

✓ Communication means that you are persuasive and objective. This is crucial when trying to get other people's objectives.

✓ Influence such that you can persuade others but still offer support to them and are trustworthy. You are able to build a consensus through a clear presentation of a case and persuading others to accept what you are offering, with a goal in mind.

✓ Developing others through giving each member of your team an opportunity to develop them and offering positive feedback. Noting other team members' achievements and strengths and rewarding them where it is due.

✓ Leadership skills that others are willing to follow you and you can delegate duties fairly and make them accountable for their actions.

✓ Change catalyst—Being able to come up with new ideas that will enable you to achieve your objective. You can spot barriers and come up with resolutions to get rid of them.

✓ Teamwork and collaboration — You can create a cohesive team that demonstrates your value for their contributions and make each and every one of them understand the objective.

All these competencies work hand in hand. Being able to understand your emotional intelligence requires you to know what you are looking for and how far you are and still have to go. The Emotional Intelligence Appraisal test is a sure way to know which skills you lack and which skills you are good at.

The next chapters in the book will show you the strategies that can be used to improve your emotional intelligence level in all the four elements of emotional intelligence; social awareness, self-management; relationship management and self-awareness.

Chapter 4

Self-Awareness Strategies

Self- awareness is:

- ✓ The ability to understand other people's emotions and know when to react and how to react to certain situations. This is a key component when it comes to relationship management. The bond that you build with others over a period of time is relationship management.

- ✓ Knowing what you are feeling at that precise moment, and using what you know to guide your decision making. Have a well-grounded sense of confidence and realistic assessment of your abilities.

Understanding your emotions and other people's emotions as well so that you can have better interactions is self-awareness. This goes hand in hand with clear communication and handling of conflicts effectively.

To have a better understanding of yourself is being able to peel back the layers that make you and being comfortable with what is in the middle. You need to know the full range of your emotions, both the negative and positive emotions.

Emotions have a strange way of resurfacing when they are not understood and noticed. This is a means of letting you know that something needs your immediate attention. It takes a lot of energy and one being honest with oneself in order to get in touch with your emotions.

There are 15 strategies that help you to create positive impacts in your life.

1. *Observing the Ripple Effect from Your Emotions*- An outpour of your emotions is like a stone that ripples through people. Your behavior is mainly influenced by your emotions, therefore understanding the effect you have on people is important.

An example can be when a manager berates an employee in front of other employees. The one affected isn't the one being berated but the other employees too as they are afraid of doing something that will make them a target. This then makes them play safe and not take risks, only doing what is expected of them.

To fully grasp how your emotions affect others:

- ✓ Watch how they react immediately and use it as a guide to know how your emotions affect a larger group of people once you've let go.

- ✓ You can ask other people how they are affected by your emotions.

- ✓ Spend some time reflecting on your behavior.

The type of ripples you want to create all depends on how well you understand your emotions.

2. *Watch Yourself Like a Hawk* – This is by developing an objective outlook on your behavior. You can achieve this by taking note of your thoughts, behavior, and emotions as a situation unfolds. The goal of doing this is to allow yourself to slow down and observe what is going on and allow your brain to process this information.

3. *Don't let a Bad Mood Fool you* – A dark cloud always forms over your feelings and thoughts when things don't go exactly as we want them to. It affects whatever it is you are currently experiencing. When this

happens, we are most likely to lose sight of what is good in our lives and focus on the bad. This can trickle down to you hating your job, being annoyed by your friends and your outlook of the future being dampened.

Self-awareness is all about knowing that you can't change a situation but you know what is going on. Bear in mind that emotions change and the dark cloud won't last.

Understand what is causing your dark mood and make decisions that will help you pull out of the mood. Do not make important decisions at such a time.

4. *Ask Why you do What you do* – Find out where your feelings came from. Ask yourself where some emotions came from making you act out of character. If you take the time to ask yourself why you feel the way you do, you will realize what is going on within you.

A little practice can help you trace the beginning of your emotions and understand the purpose of the emotions. This strategy is a good way of improving your self-awareness skill. Ask if the same emotion came when you were with someone and the situation you were in; does it relate to all the current situation or is it, specific people. You will get better at keeping your emotions in check once you understand the situations that caused your emotions.

5. *Check Yourself-* How you look is a reflection of how you feel. Your posture, demeanor, facial expressions and clothes all say important things about how you feel. Physical appearance is more straightforward as what you wear portrays your mood. Like over dressing might come off as you trying too hard, sweatpants and disheveled hair state that you have given up.

Demeanor says a lot about you but it can be misinterpreted. For instance, when meeting someone for the first time, and you are insecure about how you will be perceived. You might come off aloof or overzealous.

When you are in similar situations often, take note of your emotions and consider their influence on your demeanor. Before a mood sets the tone for the day ahead of you, check that you are okay and have control over your emotions. This is one way of understanding how and what you truly feel.

6. *Journal Your Emotions* – Having a hard day, every day, might make it difficult for you to objectify your

emotions properly. To help you overcome this, journal what triggers every strong emotion and how you respond or react to them.

Write about everything, when you were at home or at work. Within a month, you will develop a better understanding and see a pattern in your emotions. You will be able to note which emotions you cannot tolerate, pick you up or make you feel down.

Make sure to pay attention to what triggers your emotions and push your buttons. Describe in detail how you feel each day and the physical sensations accompanying the emotion. The journal is a great reference as you raise your self-awareness. The triggers and tendencies are displayed clearly for you to keep track of.

7. *Know what and who Pushes Your Buttons* – We have pet peeves, triggers that irritate you till you want to explode. Knowing what and who pushes you and how they do it is one way of maintaining your poise and get to calm yourself and be able to control such situations.

Make a note of situations and people that specifically trigger your emotions. A large number of people might trigger your emotions, be it drama queens, getting caught off guard or noisy offices. Understanding the situations that make you have strong emotions makes it less of a surprise in case it happens.

You can go further by trying to figure out why these specific situations and people trigger your emotions while others like them or worse do not. Write a list of things that push your buttons.

8. *Don't Categorize Your Emotions as Bad or Good* – Putting a label on your emotions makes it difficult for you to fully understand what it is you are feeling. Sitting on an emotion and fully becoming aware of it helps you understand what causes it.

Judging what you are feeling the way you are feeling adds more emotions to what you are already feeling. Suspending judgment on emotions makes them vanish in the end. Take notice of the next emotion that you feel immediately and understand that it is trying to show you something important.

9. *Lean into Your Discomfort* – Avoiding your discomfort merely makes it a huge problem later on. You do not manage yourself if you cannot be comfortable with what you need to change.

What you need to do is go towards what you are feeling, be in it to understand it better, then go through it. Ignoring an emotion is worse as they tend to creep up when you least expect them to. In order to be effective in life, we need to discover what things we term as unimportant and don't want to learn about.

Once you learn to lean into your discomfort, you learn that it reaps rewards. You get to know what you should do to change the way you are feeling and how to move on from an emotion.

10. *Get to Feel Your Emotions Physically* – The physical sensation includes increased heart rate, mouth going dry, or your breath quickening. Understand the physical sensations that accompany your emotions.

The next time you are alone, close your eyes. Note the rate of your breathing; whether your heart rate is fast or slow; how tense your muscles are. Think of a situation that triggered strong emotions in you— both negative and positive situations — and take note of your physical sensations.

Try not to think too hard when trying to figure out how you are feeling physically. After a while, you will be able to identify an emotion way before it begins to happen.

11. *Do let a Good Mood Fool you* – A good or bad mood can deceive your thinking. It is something most people do when excited, spend! This is common, especially after pay-day. Being in a good mood can make you make impulsive decisions that make you ignore the repercussions that will happen later on.

Impulsive decisions are bound to come from good moods; therefore, be cautious about how your good moods make you react. This will help you not regret being in a good mood next time.

12. *Pay Your Values a Visit* – Maintaining your job, school work, bills, social life, and other things take the attention away from inside you to the outside world. You tend to forget your values and beliefs when you are trying to keep a balancing act on all your outward aspects.

As a result, you might find yourself saying and doing things that do not reflect who you are. The way to handle this is by jotting down your core values and beliefs. Get to ask yourself what are your core values that you want to live your life by.

On a piece of paper, separate it into two columns and write your values and beliefs on the right and on the left what you have done that you are not proud of. Take note of what does not go with what you have noted down.

Repeat this process daily or monthly to help you boost your self-awareness. You will eventually think before you act.

13. *Seek Feedback* – There is a chasm between the way you view yourself and how people view you that has lessons that can build your self-awareness.

Open yourself to feedback from other people, like friends, mentor, and family. Look for similarities from the information that you get and also ask for examples. This will help put into perspective how your emotions affect those around you. Few achieve it, but you can gather up the courage to know what others see in you.

14. *Spot Your Emotions in Music, Movies, and Books* – If you cannot pin point your emotion patterns, look at movies, books or music you like.

Looking into them can provide a tool for you to express your emotions to others and they can teach you a lot about yourself.

When you get a glimpse of what you are feeling, it is better to show it to someone when you cannot put it in words. Look closely into what you are watching or listening to, you might be surprised at what you find out.

15. *Get to Know What you are like Under Stress*— Most of us tend to have an inkling of when stress is approaching but are you among the few that take note of the warning?

Learn to recognize your first stress sign like an upset stomach can be nervousness and the fatigue that follows is a way of your body telling you to rest. Take time to listen to your body and the signals it sends so as to recharge your emotional battery before stress causes permanent damage to you.

Chapter 5

Self-Management Strategies

This is the effective use of your awareness to your emotions and choosing what you do and say. To influence what is really going on underneath the surface, there are several things that you can do.

Self-awareness is a buildup to self-management. You can react or respond to an emotion only if you know what that emotion is. Having a high-level self-management is by ensuring that you are not standing in the way of your own success by doing things that limit it.

When you understand your emotions better, you are likely to take control of situations that are difficult or seem to bring out the worst emotions in you. Flexibility comes in when it seems to you that the direction you are heading towards, based on your emotions is wrong. It also helps you to choose a positive way of handling situations or how you react to them.

Take some time in your busy life to ponder on your feelings and how many roles do they play in influencing your behavior. When you don't do this, there is the likelihood of you being a victim of emotional hijacking.

Ways to help you manage your emotions include:

1. Make your goals public – When you share with friends or family what you are trying to accomplish there is a sense of accountability as they are aware of your progress.

When you think of other people's expectations of you and what you are doing, it tends to get you off the proverbial couch. Select people who will keep track of your progress and ask them to hold you accountable. They can also have rewards and punishment if you do not complete your task.

2. Sleep on it – At times we do not practice patience when handling a situation. The wait makes us uncomfortable and we jump into action to alleviate the tension we are experiencing.

Most of the time, waiting it out through giving yourself a day, week or month before acting can be what we need to stay in control of the situation. Time helps you to gain control of emotions that will most likely lead you to the wrong direction if you let them.

Wait before jumping in:

3. Set time for problem-solving – We all experience different emotions or feelings throughout the day, one emotion to the next fast. This can cause us to make inappropriate decisions.

Some decisions are made when rushing through the day and not when clearly thought through. Set some time aside in your day for problem-solving. Shutdown your computer, put away your phone and just think. This will help you not to use your emotions to make crucial decisions.

4. Less focus on intimidations but on your freedoms – Whenever you feel like you do not have control of a situation; take a closer look as to how you are reacting to the situation.

Do not focus on the restrictions as they can be demoralizing and most likely negative feelings will surface increasing your helplessness. Be accountable for what you can control and focus the remaining energy on being open-minded and flexible no matter what is going on.

5. Accept that change is right around the corner — by being prepared for change. By thinking through the

consequences that might occur due to changes to avoid being caught off-guard.

It is best to acknowledge that not everything in your life is under your control. Businesses ebb away, people change, things don't always stay the same. You are likely not to be shocked when you allow yourself to anticipate change.

When you experience negative changes, your attitude of acceptance makes it possible for you to think rationally when thinking of unforeseen situations.

To accomplish this, make it a duty to list down, on a weekly basis, important changes that are most likely to happen and leave space for what you will potentially do in case the change occurs. Also, write the ideas for things that can be done immediately in preparation for the change.

You become a more flexible and adaptable person when you do this, even if what you have written down does not come true.

6. Learn from people you meet – Approaching people like they have something that can impact your life makes you more open-minded, less stressed and flexible.

You are more likely not to get easily annoyed or angry when you are trying to learn something from other people. When you get to realize you are being defensive, take that opportunity to learn from the other person's feedback or how they are behaving.

7. Stay synchronized – The emotions that you are portraying and your body language go hand in hand. Your emotions get the better of you when your body language is not in check.

Focus on the situation you are going through and not your emotions.

8. Make your sleep hygiene clean – Having a good night sleep is critical in our lives. It makes you focused, alert and have a balanced mind. To have better sleep:

- Twenty minutes before you sleep, turn your computer off. The light from the computer resembles that of the sun and your brain is tricked into thinking it is morning. It is difficult to sleep after being on your laptop for long and immediately going to sleep.

- Avoid caffeine as it has a six-hour half-life. It will keep you awake because it is disruptive to your sleep. It should be taken only before noon and in small quantities.

- Twenty minutes of morning sunlight helps to reset your inner clock. You get to sleep easily in the evening.

- Make sure your bed is only for sleeping and not for watching television or watching movies. Your body will respond when you only use your bed for sleeping.

9. Laugh and smile more – Force yourself to have a positive reaction, like smiling when you are dealing with a difficult situation. This counteracts the negative emotions you are having.

You can lift your mood by reading or watching something humorous. You get to override negative emotions bothering you and have a clear mind.

10. Count to ten – When getting frustrated, close your eyes and count to ten. Take a deep breath and exhale while you count one in your head. The breathing and counting are to help you relax and not make rash decisions or take rash actions.

It provides the right amount of time for you to look at your situation differently. You can have a drink in hand, stress ball if you do not want people to notice what you are doing.

It is easy to have an emotional comeback that will later result in a heated argument that you could have prevented. Slowing down makes you take the situation into perspective and you get to regain control of yourself and prevent emotions from running loose.

11. Reason versus emotions list – You get to have a clear mind then focus on what your emotions are saying without letting them decide what to do next.

From the list, question why your reason is ignoring what your emotions are trying to say. Then figure out why your judgment is being clouded by your emotions. The list will help you determine whether the reason or emotional side of you has more say.

12. Have a chat with a skilled self-manager – who might be your role model and get to learn some, if not all, of their tricks. You might know a person or you can have them take the Appraisal test to know if they are.

You can take them out for coffee or a meal and explain your situation to them. Let them know you're aims of improving your self-management and ask them how they do theirs. From the tips you have received, select those that you will use immediately.

13. Visualize yourself succeeding – Visualizing yourself handling your behavior and emotions better is a way to practice your skills and transform them into a habit.

Close your eyes while in bed and visualize how you handled a situation during the day that made you react in a way that was out of your control. Then think of how you should have reacted.

Visualize yourself saying and doing the right things and have some satisfaction from what you have just thought of. Incorporate this nightly with more challenging situations each time.

14. Involve someone who isn't emotionally invested in your problem – Another perspective might be what you need to see things differently. The person you are talking to should care about how you are feeling.

Seek someone who is not emotionally affected by your situation, when you have a difficult situation. Their perspective will widen your options and have another view of what is going on.

15. Have a mental recharge session in your schedule – when you get to relax your mind. Exercising is a crucial activity that not only recharges your mind but also relieves you of some stress.

Taking time to exercise recharges your brain before you sleep. You can do yoga, have a massage, stroll through a park, all are ways to relax your mind.

Finding time to squeeze in these activities is the hard part. In the beginning of the week, make them part of your schedule instead of waiting to have time for them.

16. Take control of your self-talk – The most influential talks are those that we literally talk to ourselves. When you experience an emotion, it is common for your thoughts to turn the heat up or down. Learning to control self-talk can help you remain focused on the right things around you and you also get to manage your emotions more effectively.

- Say "sometimes" instead of "I never". Each situation should be treated individually and do not beat yourself up about what has already happened.

- Try to avoid saying "I am an idiot" but be objective about what you have done by acknowledging that you have made a mistake. You focus solely on what you can change about your situation.

- Don't point fingers and accept responsibility for your mistakes.

17. Do breathe correctly – Your brain is deprived of oxygen when you take small, shallow breaths. It can result in forgetfulness and lack of energy.

Take deep breaths and exhale with your mouth. This is a breathing exercise you can do when in a stressful situation. Whether you are in a fixated situation or negative thoughts are churning in your brain, make yourself breathe right and you will calm down.

Chapter 6

Social-Awareness Strategies

Getting to recognize and understand people's moods and groups is social awareness. This is appreciating other people and you willing to learn from them. To build your social-awareness skill, you are likely to observe other people in various settings.

You might be in line waiting to be served or seated on a park bench observing someone from afar. Check their facial expression, the tone of their voice, or body language. Having an astute social awareness skill might come in handy wherever you are.

To become more socially aware, you need to give your full attention to the person or people you are with. You utilize all your five senses and the information that you are gathering from using your sixth sense, your emotions are being utilized as well. The emotions play an important role as they can help you to take cues from others.

There are 17 strategies that can help you to handle different situations that you may encounter.

1. **See the Whole Picture** – Seeking other people's perspective of you is key to achieving social awareness. Accept the feedback that you get from your friends, family and also some of the people you can hardly tolerate.

Other people's opinions do matter as they influence your life. The best way to achieve this is by sending a 360 survey to yourself and everyone that asks them of your self-management, self-awareness, social-awareness, and relationship management skills. It provides a clear picture of how others perceive you as well as yourself.

2. **Do a Test for Accuracy** – There are days you have an off day and you are in situations that you can't read. Ask if you are trying to justify an observation that you have made. This is through asking if what you are observing in people and/or in the situation is actually as it is.

In case a friend does not look okay, yet they have said they are fine, try and find out why by stating your evidence then ask a direct question. Like, "you seem down. Is everything okay?" There are those people who are not comfortable stating how they feel, they will drop hints. If you are comfortable asking, this is an opportunity for you to see if what you picked up on and what they were saying are the same. You will be able to note if you are jumping to conclusions or you missed some cues.

3. Take your time to understand why they behave in a particular manner by stepping into their shoes. This will help you have a deeper understanding of what they are going through and help you notice if there are problems about to happen or occur. You gain a perspective of their situation and you can communicate to them with what you have learned in mind.

You achieve this by putting away your tendencies, emotions, beliefs, thinking patterns and focus on how the person at hand feels. You can test this by approaching the person and checking if what you are thinking is on point.

4. **Go out and Watch People** – Sit on a park bench, coffee shop and just observe people milling about going on with their business. Taking this time, you will be able to observe people showing their emotions without meaning to. Watch how they interact with others in the

grocery shop or when people are going through books on shelves at the bookstore.

This can be a trial run to see if you can spot people's emotions and subtle cues as to how they feel. People-watching helps one to observe interactions, figure underlying emotions and motives and you get to pick up on signals.

Getting to learn how to pick on people's emotions and moods is key in being socially aware of what is going on around you.

5. **At the Movies, Watch for EQ** – Being aware of what is happening with other people, be it a box office movie or the people you are with at a party, you can build your social awareness skill either way.

6. **Live in the Moment** – Be a child. A child does not worry about yesterday's events or what might happen tomorrow; they live in the now unlike adults who worry about the past, present and future.

Living like a child is one way of building your social awareness skill, as you get to notice what is happening with others at that particular moment. Wherever you might be, be there and only there.

Pondering on what you did in the past and evaluating what you can do in the future is a valuable exercise but it should not be done on a daily basis as you tend to forget what is happening right in front of you, in the present.

7. **Have a Back-pocket Question** – This is a question you have that will help you move away from an awkward silence. This strategy makes you seem like you are interested in the other person's ideas, feelings, and thoughts.

It can be "what is your thought on…?" select a topic that will engage the other person and will require them to explain in detail what their opinions are. Avoid religion, politics or sensitive topics that make people uncomfortable.

It might feel like an abrupt change of subject but you get to add life to the conversation. If it doesn't work, excuse yourself to do something else or involve someone else in your conversation.

8. **Greet People who you know by Name** – This is a meaningful way of involving someone in what you are trying to say to them. By saying someone's name, you

come off as inviting and warm. It is a social strategy to call people by name.

Be sure to use the person's name at least twice during your conversation. Remembering someone's name when you meet them makes your mind focus more and also increases your awareness in social settings.

9. **Make Timing a Thing** – When you react to other people's emotions, make sure you do it at the right time. Ask questions at the right time by putting what they feel first then your curiosity.

It is all about the other person and not about you; ergo, time your question according to their frame of mind.

10. **Watch People's Body Language** – Hand movement, posture, eye movement, facial expressions all should be looked at carefully. Start with the face and head. Eye contact indicates that someone is trustworthy but when they blink several times they are deceptive. An honest and sincere person exhibits relaxed eye movements, as they still pay attention to what you are saying.

The smile will indicate if it is forced or sincere. Crinkles at the end of the eye, show it is a sincere smile. Shoulders should not be tensed or slouching, but upright; hands, feet, and legs can be either fidgety or calm. Once you master body language, you will be able to call someone's bluff.

11. **For Social Gathering Plan Ahead** – Carry a list of talking points or what to do when attending a social event like a dinner. Planning will help you enjoy the event as well as prepare you for the event itself. You won't be stressed and you get to be present while talking with other people.

12. **Take a 15-minute Tour** – Do go for a stroll around your work building or gym. This can help you note who seeks interaction, and who stays on their desks all day when people move in and out of the building.

Another day can be to observe how other people behave by taking note of what you pick, hear and see in other people.

13. **Clear the Clutter Away** – Do away with internal distractions that make you not to be aware of what is going on at the moment.

You can achieve this by:

- Not interrupting another person when they are talking until they finish.

- Not planning your response.

- Lean towards the person you are communicating with to refocus on their words.

As you clear out clutter, it will be easy for you to calm your thoughts and sharpen your listening skills.

14. **Do not make Notes at Meetings** – You tend to miss critical cues that can come from meetings that can shed light to what those around you are feeling. Focus on their body language and what their facial expressions are saying. Maintain eye contact with the person talking. You will be more engaged and focused on other people.

15. **Listen** – to the other person's volume of voice, speed, and tone. You can get to know what a speaker's state of mind is by observing the stated points above.

To put this into practice, when someone is talking, stop all that you are doing and listen fully to what they are saying. This will help you stay at present and pick on cues from people and hear what they are really trying to say.

16. **Culture Game Rules** – Stop focusing on how you should be treated but how others would like to be treated.

Open yourself to new ideas and understand what others like or don't like to avoid putting your foot in your mouth. Look for similarities that are there when you play compared to how they play the game.

Ask specific questions when having social interactions around meals.

17. **Catch the Mood in the Room** – It can be by what your gut instincts are telling you or by observing how people are interacting in the room.

You can use an experienced social aware person to tell what is going on in the room and let them show you how you can achieve the same level of social awareness that they have. It is possible for you to hone on the concerns, safety, and shifts in the moods of people in groups and know how to handle them. This will come in handy when dealing with any group setting you might encounter.

What to remember from all this is: **Focusing on other people and their tendencies and not on yours, is the key to social awareness.**

Chapter 7

Latest Discoveries in Emotional Intelligence

In recent years, EQ has been incorporated into many aspects of our lives such that employers are also looking into their employees EQ. Thousands of school across the globe offer SEL to children, with EQ being adapted into school settings.

In the United States, entire states and many districts have currently made SEL curriculum a requirement. Students must attain a certain competence level in languages and math; therefore, they should also attain the same in essential skills.

It is essential to have a high EQ level, but how vital is it in leading a healthy productive professional and personal life? Research has shed light on generation divide, battle of the sexes and quest for higher paying jobs.

This is what was concluded;

Battle of the Sexes:

There was a huge difference between the EQ skills men and women expressed according to a study done in 2003. Men could only keep pace with women in self-awareness while women outshine men in relationship management, social awareness, and self-management. But times have changed with men catching up on women in the ability to manage their own emotions. This can be attributed to change in social norms.

Men are recently encouraged to pay attention to their emotions more which helps in clear thinking. It was found that 70% of men who are the top 15% in decision making have the highest scores in EQ skills. It has been proven that paying extra attention to your emotions is a clear way of making the best decisions.

Top managers have the lowest rankings of EQ skill compared to middle managers in a workplace. This is because they spend less time interacting with their staff but more time on their computers and issuing orders without knowing what is going on in their firm. It's been proven that having a high EQ is more critical in leadership skills than any other skill.

The Difference Between EQ then and Now

In the US, between 2003 and 2007, there has been a steady climb of EQ in the US workforce. This was attributed to the number of people who are attuned to their emotions and those of others increasing from 13% to 18.3% and those who did not understand how anger or frustration influenced their behavior to reduce from 31% to 14%.

This is a unique case as these people do not have any training in emotional intelligence and how it affects our lives. The EQ skills that we require are all dependent on the circumstances and people we surround ourselves with every day.

When we spend time with people who are open to sharing their emotions, we get to learn how to be the same, and if we spend time with empathetic people, we also become empathetic towards others. EQ can be learned, it's not something that we were born with.

Under stress, we are likely to digress from the progress we made. In 2008, EQ levels dropped due to a hard time experienced; famine and economic depression. Our emotions are affected negatively on a long-term basis, making it difficult for us to move on.

The drop was from 18.3% to 16.7%, which is approximately 2 million people who could not recover from the stressful situations they underwent in 2008. These people could have been guides to many others on how to master EQ, but they were weighed down by their emotions and struggled to master their own skills.

Generational Divide; EQ and Age

To get this into perspective, generations are broken down into four generations; Generation Y (18-30 years old) Generation X (31-43 years old), Baby Boomers (43-61 years old) and Traditionalists (61-80 years old).

Between Gen Y and Baby Boomers, a huge gap is seen in self-management meaning that Baby Boomers can handle situations if they don't get their way better than the younger generation. Despite the technical know-how that the younger generation has over the older generation, the lack of self-management skill makes it difficult for them to lead and manage others.

With age, it seems that self-management increased as 60-year-olds scored higher than 50-year-olds. This means that the younger generations' deficiency in self-management is not something that can be controlled or is it due to the effects of growing up with Facebook and Instagram.

Honing EQ skills take time, but this can be cut in half with more concentration and the will to learn how to make you better. Gen Y is good at soaking up a lot of information on a short period of time. Therefore, it is up to them to either wait till they are 50 to master their skills or develop the skills on their own.

Baby Boomers are retiring soon; therefore, Gen Y must prepare to take over the leadership roles that will be left behind. This opportunity will help Gen Y make the world as they want to see it and also get good pay.

Emotional ignorance is the downfall of many people around the world. Such people are likely to have little to no understanding of how their emotions affect other people and their lives as they will have a hard time succeeding in the world.

It is of utmost importance that people learn to use the right strategies and tools to have better control of their emotions. It will increase their chances of succeeding and this applies to countries, organizations, and individuals.

In China, EQ plays a major role in how businesses are run. The Chinese have discipline, which is something most American executives lack. American executives scored 15 points below Chinese executives in self-management and relationship management. The scores of Chinese executives were similar to those of American executives in self-awareness and social awareness, though slightly higher.

The difference comes in where the Chinese executives use this knowledge to their advantage. Executives in China plan or schedule dinner to discuss various affairs of their families, business trends, and career aspirations with their employees.

American leaders give permission to the HR on the qualities that they can put into the company competence model. They like how the behavior looks on paper but are afraid to walk the talk. When it comes to seeking feedback, US executives are likely to only offer lip service. This is also applied in following through with their commitments, getting to know their peers or working as a team.

Conclusion

EQ is a skill that can be learned and unlearned, as illustrated in the rise of EQ skilled people and drop in 2008. It is possible to sharpen your EQ skills over a period of time, but an incident can occur that dulls your skills.

It is important to read this book and many others at least once a year so that you can learn the strategies for improving your EQ skills. You cannot master golf by practicing in six months then quitting, you need to practice as often as you can to be a master at what you want to be. It might be golf, piano, or any sport, practice, practice and more practice. It is easy to lose these hard-earned skills as easily as you learned them.

Make sure that you study and identify your areas of weakness to be able to know where you can make changes. Acknowledging that you have low emotional intelligence skills or none whatsoever, is the first step in the right direction. Make sure you do the Emotional Intelligence Appraisal Test to help you identify what skills you lack. Use the strategies in this book to guide you through your skills and make you master them, one skill at a time.

What you need to do next is start putting in place all that you have read in this book into practice immediately! If you find it a bit difficult to remember all that you have read, start a skill at a time to maximize your potential. Breaking down each skill and going through the strategies provided for each skill will make it easy for you to attain a high score level on that particular emotional intelligence skill.

Empath

How To Protect Yourself From Negativity
And Thrive As An Empath

Written by

George Muntau

The information in the following pages is broadly considered to be a truthful and accurate account of facts, and as such any inattention, use or misuse of the information in question by the reader will render any resulting actions solely under their purview. There are no scenarios in which the publisher or the original author of this work can be in any fashion deemed liable for any hardship or damages that may befall them after undertaking information described herein.

Additionally, the information found on the following pages is intended for informational purposes only and should thus be considered, universal. As befitting its nature, the information presented is without assurance regarding its continued validity or interim quality. Trademarks mentioned are done without written consent and can in no way be considered an endorsement from the trademark holder.

Introduction

Empathy vs. Empaths

Congratulations on purchasing your personal copy of "Empath: How To Protect Yourself From Negativity And Thrive As An Empath". Thank you for doing so.

The following chapters of this book will discuss some of the ways you can learn the difference between basic empathy and being an empath, protect yourself from negativity, and thrive with your personality type. The final chapter will explore tips and tricks for making the most out of life and yourself.

Empathy vs. Empaths— Important Differences

Being empathetic means being able to relate to the people around you and their emotions and thoughts, and most humans have this, but this is not the same as being an empath.

A Spiritual Term

Empath is basically another word for being clairsentient. With this term, you are moving into the world of spirituality and away from the world of basic psychology. Up to 4 percent of humans are clairsentient in some way.

Why does the distinction between being empathetic and being an actual empath really matter? It matters because if you're an empath, you need special considerations and tools to handle this ability without becoming overwhelmed or overstressed.

Labels Allow Understanding

Labels are important because they allow us to both seek the understanding we require to thrive in life and help get the support we need. It also helps you develop a sense of self. Everyone has various categories and labels that they fall into and this is just another way to understand yourself.

The Discomfort Of Being An Empath

Another reason why the distinction between empathy and empaths matter is because addressing the ability of empaths can be uncomfortable. It can be tempting to hide away the skill of heightened empathy in order to fit into the world better or judge ourselves less. This is because many empaths are raised to be okay with the idea of being sensitive, but clairsentient is a bigger leap. It's much easier to think that you are perceptive with body language and good at interpreting facial expressions than to believe that you have some kind of special intuitive ability that most others don't.

Changing Your Worldview As An Empath

Accepting that you are an empath means that you may have to make some changes to the way you currently see the world. So what does this look like in practice? Here are some examples of ideas you may need to come to terms with in order to proceed on the path to fully understand yourself:

- **Energy:** In order to accept the premise of being an empath, you need to come to terms with the fact that energy is perceivable and real, something that can be picked up with your other senses. This can be hard to accept, and many are skeptical, but as soon as you see it, it's impossible to ignore and helps everything make a lot more sense.

- **Emotions:** Physical sensations and emotions are forms of energy that are equally powerful. In fact, it may help to think of them as one and the same.

- **The Transfer Of Both:** Energy, including emotions, is something that can be transferred, stuck to you, blended with other energies, and can even be thrown around.

Thinking in the classic way of psychology, this might only seem symbolic. However, if you know that you are truly an empath, this is going to be real for you, and if you ignore it, you're going to have a harder time than necessary. Anytime someone is stuck in your mind as an empath, this is not only in your mind.

You probably have very real subconscious exchanges of energy happening between you and them. When someone deeply impacts you, as an empath, it isn't just having a vivid imagination of what they are going through; you are literally sensing their emotions.

How This Book Will Help You

When you're an empath, regardless of how much you may try to change your own mood, sometimes you just can't. Even when you've done all the right things to move beyond something, you may still feel stuck. This isn't because you're only thinking about or merely empathizing with others, but literally taking on their energy. This is why training yourself to handle your abilities is so important. It is tailored to your situation and goes above and beyond basic psychological tips for coping. This book will help you find these tools.

There are plenty of books on this subject on the market, thanks again for choosing this one! Every effort was made to ensure it is full of as much useful information as possible. Please enjoy!

Chapter 1

What Makes An Empath?
Traits And Signs

Many people are fascinated by the subject of empathy because they can tell that the world needs more of it. Empathy is what happens when we relate to others with our hearts instead of our minds, putting ourselves in their position and feeling with them. But being an empath is different and takes it further. Empaths exist very high on the spectrum of empathy and don't just imagine what it's like to be in another's shoes; they feel with them. This results in them having amazing compassion for others, but it can get heavy and overwhelming. This is why developing healthy strategies to guard their own sensitivities is so important.

Being Taken Advantage Of

Every empath knows what it's like to be taken advantage of. Their sensitive, understanding disposition makes them a target for people who want to dump all their issues on them. This is why protecting yourself and coming up with healthy boundaries matters so much. One of the first steps to understanding your own gifts is realizing where they come from. Let's look at some scientific explanations for heightened empathy and empaths.

Mirror Neurons

Scientists have found a specific brain cell grouping that gives us compassion. These cells are responsible for mirror emotions, allowing us to share someone else's joy, fear, or pain. Since empaths are believed to possess very sensitive mirror neurons, they resonate deeply with the emotions of others. How does that happen? Outside events trigger the mirror neurons in the brain. For instance, when you see your spouse get hurt, you feel it, as well. If your kid is upset, you are also sad. When your friend receives good news, you are also happy.

On the other end of the spectrum, narcissists, sociopaths, and psychopaths are severely lacking in this and have an empathy deficient. In other words, they don't have the ability to empathize the way most others do, and this might be because their mirror neurons are under-active. These people should be approached with caution, especially for empaths. We will talk a bit more about how to protect yourself from negativity in chapter three.

Contagious Emotions

Another observation that has helped the scientific understanding of empaths is emotional contagion. Studies show that people soak up the feelings of the ones around them. For example, a crying baby will cause other babies to cry in a nursery. One person complaining and worrying out loud at work can cause their co-workers to also feel worried. People usually catch the emotions of others in group situations. An article published in the New York Times recently said that being able to sync our moods up to others is a must for healthy relationships.

How can empaths learn from this? By choosing positive influences in life instead of getting dragged down by pessimism and negativity. Or if a friend of yours is having a bad time, make sure you are protecting yourself and grounding yourself. These strategies will be taught throughout this book.

Electromagnetic Fields And Empaths

The third finding is about our hearts and brains generating electromagnetic fields. According to studies done by the Heart Math Institute, the fields transfer data about the emotions and thoughts of those around us. Empaths are usually sensitive to that input and get easily overwhelmed. On a similar note, empaths often experience a higher emotional and physical reaction to the sun and earth's electromagnetic fields.

Heightened Sensitivity To Dopamine

Yet another finding has to do with dopamine, the neurotransmitter related to the human pleasure response. Studies have proven that empaths that are introverted are usually also more sensitive to this neurotransmitter than people who are more extroverted. Essentially, they don't require as much dopamine to feel pleasure or happiness.

This could provide an explanation as to why they enjoy simple activities such as meditation, reading, and alone time, and don't need as much stimulation from the outside world.

On the other hand, more extroverted people crave plenty of excitement and social interaction.

The Precious Human Trait

According to the Dali Lama, empathy is our most valuable, precious quality, as humans. In times of stress, it can be easy to lose hope or feel overwhelmed, which makes empathy all the more important as this helps us get through the hard times. It allows us to respect each other, even in times of disagreement. Contrary to what some believe, high empathy doesn't make you too sentimental or keep you from practicing accurate judgment rather, it lets you reach a higher understanding of others by opening your heart. It doesn't always work for creating more peace and reaching others, but if we have a shot, empathy is it.

The Empath, Defined

If you're an empath, it means you're deeply affected by the energies of those around you and can sense and feel other people intuitively. Your daily life is influenced unconsciously by the moods, thoughts, wishes, and desires of those around you. If you're an empath, it means more than simply being sensitive, and has more to it than just being related to emotions. Empaths are able to pick up on spiritual urges and sensitivities, along with knowing the intentions and motivations of others. Either you're this type of person, or you are not. This trait cannot be learned the way that basic empathy can.

Traits Of The Empath

An empath is always open to processing others' energies and feelings. What this means is that they really take on and feel the feelings of other people. A lot of empaths will go through periods of unexplained aches, environmental sensitivities, or chronic fatigue. Most likely, these are all related to the influences outside of you rather than just yourself. Basically, you're going through life and experiencing all of the accumulated energy, emotions, and karma from those around you. It's a lot to handle! Here are some other traits related to empaths:

- High Achievers: Empaths are great achievers and are often very humble and quiet about it. Empaths can be slow to accept compliments and would rather point out the positive qualities of other people. They are good at expressing themselves in emotional situations and like to talk in an open and frank way. Unlike many people, empaths find it easy to share their thoughts and feelings.

- Unresponsive Sometimes: Even though empaths are very caring and empathetic, of course, they may also be the opposite at times. Actually, they may be seen as unresponsive and even reclusive, seeming ignorant to others. This is because they have a hard time sometimes with being overwhelmed by emotions and instead decide to keep to themselves.

- Ignoring Personal Needs: Empaths are great at picking up on the feelings and thoughts outside of them. At times, they may be so caught up on this that they ignore what's going on inside, meaning that their own needs don't always get met. Usually, empaths are non-aggressive and non-violent, helping others make peace. Situations that are awkward or tense make the empath feel very uncomfortable, meaning that they may attempt to either avoid or walk away from situations that fit this description.

- Building Barriers: Empaths might sense the feelings of others and project those emotions back to themselves without knowing or realizing where it came from. Being able to discuss these things is a huge help when it comes to releasing emotions for the empath. However, some empaths may hide their feelings and create huge barriers so that others don't know their inner feelings and thoughts. This could have to do with how they were raised or difficult emotional situations from their past. This type of withholding, emotionally, can be bad for the empath, causing the emotions to build and build to a dangerous degree. The emotions and thoughts can eventually get crippling or even explosive.

Sensitive To The News And Movies

Empaths are very sensitive, which is no secret, but this can be true even of fiction or the news. Emotional drama or violence that shows emotional or physical difficulties and pain can be hard for an empath to watch and often makes them cry. They may hide their tears or even feel sick.

Most empaths find it impossible to understand cruelty and might have a hard time sharing their true feelings with someone who doesn't understand this. They find it hard to relate to others that do not have a strong sense of compassion. Let's look at some other traits that you will find in the average empath.

Working With Nature, Animals, Or People

Empaths often work with nature, animals, or people with strong dedication and a true sense of passion for helping the world. They are caretakers and teachers, enjoying giving up their own time to help other people, even if it means volunteering or being recognized.

Great At Telling Stories

Empaths are often great at telling stories because of their sense of imagination, expanding knowledge, and curious minds. They are often gentle and romantic at heart. In addition, they like to listen to and collect stories about their families and the ones to pass them along.

Musically Eclectic

Empaths usually have a wide interest in music and like to listen to many different types to fit their varying moods. Lyrics can be a powerful influencer for empaths. Be careful with what you listen to because it has a strong effect on your mood.

Artistically Expressive

Empaths are highly expressive with art, just as they are expressive with feelings, thoughts, and words. They express this creativity with bodily movements, acting, and dance. Empaths can send a lot of energy when they release or portray feelings, and this has a powerful impact on others. They may become easily lost in their surroundings, or music, leading them to feel as though they are one with the music.

Easy To Get Along With

Animals and many different types of people are attracted to empaths for their genuine compassion and warmth. Even if they can't explain exactly why they are so drawn to them, people always flock to empaths and want to be around them.

Strangers find themselves sharing very personal details about themselves without planning to do so because they can tell that the empath will listen with true understanding and compassion.

Great Listeners

Empaths are life's greatest listeners. They are often enthusiastic, bubbly, and outgoing and can be very humorous, even in an unusual situation. On the other hand, an empath can feel the weight of others' moods and feel very sad. The feelings and thoughts that empaths take in from the world around them can seem very overwhelming if they don't understand what's happening. The speed with which their moods change can be worrying to them.

Curious Thinkers

Empaths are usually students of various subjects, they are thinkers and great problem solvers. The empath often believes that wherever a problem exists, an answer must also exist. They might look and look for one just to get some peace, which can be a great quality, particularly in relationships or at work. Empaths have a special connection with Universal

Knowledge, leading them to solve anything they truly wish to solve.

Vivid Dreamers

Empaths are usually lucid dreamers with many lucid experiences. They are curious about their dreams and have highly detailed dream experiences. They might have a feeling that their dreams are connected to the physical world in a way, rather than just believing that they are meaningless or nonsensical images. This belief could lead some empaths to be great at dream interpretation, both for themselves and other people.

The Daydreaming Empath

Empaths are often known as daydreamers and might have a hard time keeping their attention on anything that seems mundane to them. If an empath is not stimulated by their environment, they will go into their own mind to find something interesting. If an empath doesn't have a teacher that interests them, they may find their own way to interact with the knowledge and teach themselves.

However, if an empath has a teacher who uses emotion to teach, they will instantly be intrigued and receptive to the information.

Synchronicities And Déjà Vu

Empaths are no stranger to synchronicities and déjà vu experiences. They might begin with thinking that they are just prone to experiencing a lot of coincidence before realizing that synchronicities are deeply ingrained in who they truly are as a person. The synchronicities eventually turn into a welcomed occurrence. As they grow to understand themselves more, they will see more and more of these small signs. Eventually, these signals might make the empath feel very euphoric.

Paranormal Beliefs And Experiences

Empaths are very likely to have paranormal beliefs and experiences in life including out of body experiences and near death experiences. People who are caught up pursuing a life they don't want and work that doesn't fulfill them may be stuck in a meaningless existence. They may ignore signals of guidance and instead choose to keep doing what they usually do. This is how empaths can truly help the world; through showing that finding meaning in life is essential for health and happiness.

Experiences like the ones listed above may seem dramatic, confusing, and even life-changing. But they are there to guide you and show you who you are and what you are meant for on this earth. The next crucial area to be aware of, as an empath, is the need to take care of yourself. Let's look at some considerations related to this.

The Need To Be Heard

When the empath gets abandoned during a hard mood, it can hit them very hard. The empath simply craves compassion and listening without condemnation, bias, or judgment. These simple things can help an empath recover very quickly as they are resilient types. Most empaths go through their lives without understanding why they are the way they are and might actually feel bad about their traits.

They might feel things without realizing that the emotions are not their own, but they have simply "caught" them from someone else. This could lead them to confusion since they might feel extremely happy one moment and depressed the next.

More Traits Of The Empath

For some people with this personality type, a lack of understanding about their experiences may cause them to suppress their skills. They might even get embarrassed to feel as much as they do. Let's look at some more qualities of the empath, so you can better understand yourself.

Knowledge

Empaths simply know things, even when they are not told. It's a knowledge that is beyond gut feelings or even intuition, although this may be how it's described. The more you accept and tap into your empathetic nature, the more you will experience this gift.

Easily Overwhelmed

Empaths will get overwhelmed easily, especially when they are in crowds. Being in stadiums, supermarkets, or shopping malls can make an empath want to run and hide due to all of the emotions flying around.

Taking On Emotions

Feeling the emotions of others and mistaking them for yours is a common occurrence for the average empath. Some may even feel the emotions of those close to them as well as the emotions of those far from them, particularly when it's someone close to them.

Heightened Lie Detection

The empath can almost always tell when someone is lying. If a loved one or friend is lying to you and you are aware of this, it can be very painful. However, this is a great skill to have because you can protect yourself from expectations or getting hurt.

Chapter 2

The Challenges And Defenses Of An Empath

Being a successful empath is similar to being a success with anything else. You first have to realize, accept, and embrace the fact that you have this personality type. As soon as you can do this, the door is open to being more self-aware when it comes to your feelings and thoughts.

Empath Challenges And Traits

Empaths are always looking for the truth, even when it's hard to find. This is even truer when they discover their birthright and natural gifts. After this, any encounters with less than the truth are wrong and hard to handle. They are constantly seeking knowledge and answers to their questions. If they have questions that haven't been answered, it can be extremely disconcerting and frustrating, leading them to seek out an answer at any costs.

Also, if they have a hunch or intuitive knowing about a subject, they will make sure they seek out confirmation of their suspicion. The one downside to this attitude is that they might end up with an overabundance of information that overwhelms them. Let's look at some other traits.

Feeling Physical Symptoms

Empaths don't only pick up the emotions of others but will often pick up physical symptoms, as well. If someone else has aches, pains, or a cold, the empath will almost feel as though they also do, especially if it's someone close to them.

Back And Digestive Issues

Empaths might experience lower back and digestive issues throughout their lives. This is because of the solar plexus chakra, a chakra that exists in the abdomen and holds all emotion. Chakras are spinning wheels of energy that exist throughout the body (which we will discuss more in chapter five), and if they are not in proper balance, this can cause issues. This is where you will sense the incoming feelings of other people, and you can develop issues in the area if you don't know you are an empath or take precautions to ground yourself.

Takes The Underdog's Side

The empath will always be rooting for an underdog over the more popular one. When an empath sees someone being bullied or in emotional pain, they can't help but feel compassion and pay attention. They will also do anything to help.

People Are Open With Them

Empaths are very familiar with others being completely comfortable sharing personal things with them. Strangers will often want to open up to the empath, meaning that the empath can become a door mat if they don't know how to set healthy boundaries and look out for themselves.

They Are Often Tired

Empaths may have a habit of taking on a lot from other people and end up feeling tired as a result. They get so exhausted that even sleeping for long periods of time doesn't seem to help. This is yet another reason why knowing how to set healthy boundaries and center yourself is important.

Addictive Habits

Sex, drugs, and alcohol are all dangers that an empath can fall into addictive relationships with if they are not careful. This is their way of unloading the stress of their lives or of covering up their overwhelmed reactions to feeling everyone else's emotions so clearly and strongly.

Natural Healers

Empaths are attracted to healing careers and other metaphysical subjects. Even though a lot of empaths would thrive with healing other people, they might avoid this type of situation because it can hurt them if they don't know proper protection techniques. This is true especially if the empath is not aware of their special personality and skills. Supernatural events and subjects fascinate empaths, and they are never shocked or surprised very easily by related materials.

Solitary Animal Lovers

Empaths like to be around animals and animals also love them. In addition, they have to be alone on a regular basis, or they might start feeling over overworked and stressed out.

During this alone time, they often go for creative activities that can give them an outlet for their creative expression and the stress of feeling so much all the time.

Easily Bored Or Distracted

Empaths will get bored very quickly if they are in an environment that doesn't stimulate them. Home, school, and work life need to be interesting, or the empath will start going off in his or her own world, doodling or daydreaming. In addition, empaths find it painful or even impossible to follow through on activities they don't like. If they do this, they feel as though they are being fake. This may lead some empaths to be thought of as lazy by others who don't understand.

Adventure Seekers

Empaths are natural adventure seekers and love to travel and see new places. They are often called free spirits because they feel weighed down by obligation and would rather have the freedom to move around at will. If they cannot travel in real life, they will use their imaginations to go where they wish to go and live the lives they wish to live. In addition, their free spirits make it so that they feel imprisoned by control, rules, and routine. A lifestyle with too much of these elements will eventually suffocate the empath or cause them to be very unhappy.

They Make Great Friends

Empaths are good at listening, as mentioned earlier, and this makes them amazing, and much appreciated friends. Empaths will not talk about their own issues unless someone asks who genuinely cares. Usually, they would rather be a listening ear for those around them, friends or strangers.

Intolerant Of Narcissistic Attitudes

Empaths are some of the most tolerant people around, but they can't stand to be around arrogance or overly narcissistic people. Since empaths always put other people first, it's hard to relate to those who don't.

Noticing What Others Don't

Empaths often notice what others don't, including sensing which day it is. Empaths can feel that it is Friday, even if they forgot to check out their calendar. In addition, they will sense what others are feeling, so if people are getting overly down about being back at work on Monday, empaths will sense this, even if they don't have to work that day.

Might Seem Cold

Empaths may seem disconnected, aloof, shy, or moody to certain onlookers. They will show their moods on their faces and have a very hard time faking what they feel. Empaths may be susceptible to sudden mood changes if they have been around a lot of negativity and may seem miserable, unsociable, or quiet to those around them. Empaths hate pretending to feel okay when they don't, which means that service jobs are not always well suited for them.

How To Become Aware As An Empath

In order to use your empath gifts, you must figure out how to tell emotions apart, meaning your own emotions apart from other emotions, and the feelings of others apart from your own feelings. This will require practice and plenty of time and effort.

Clearing Out Excess Emotion

Anytime you have a feeling, ask yourself if you are feeling it because of an event in your life, or if you are picking up on something that is coming from outside of you. Any time you notice yourself picking up on other people's emotions, set up a clear emotional boundary between you and their situation and pause to clear out the feeling. The more you practice this, the easier it gets.

Pay Attention To Your Feelings

Feelings, just like physical sensations, are there for a reason. They are meant to help us make decisions and navigate our lives. If you accidentally burn yourself on a hot pan, you will no longer touch hot pans. In a similar way, if you find that a situation continuously harms you on an emotional level, you will learn to avoid situations like that. Being an empath means that you have a highly attuned and advanced inner guidance system in terms of emotion. But in order to make use of this, you have to first realize how important your emotions really are.

Becoming An Empowered Individual

Being an empath can be stressful in and of itself because you need unique adjustments that others may not. Your ultimate goal should be to become an empowered individual, empathetic gifts and all. This means you must become more proactive with your life situation. As soon as you learn to notice your feelings and recognize how to use them to point you in the right direction, you are heading in the right direction.

- Adjusting Your Life: Your heightened sensitivity helps you to stay away from negative or overwhelming environments and work with your personality to create the life you want. If you know that crowded situations make you uncomfortable, you can adjust your life to only hang out with smaller groups. If waiting until the last minute for work deadlines gives you anxiety, you could make sure you always start your projects early.

- Planning Ahead: Since you have the unique gift of picking up on the emotions of other people, you can plan ahead with your life to help others with their needs. For instance, if your best friend is getting nervous about a test they have the next day, instead of picking up on their anxiety (which doesn't help them much), you could instead make them dinner that night, so they have more study time.

As you can see, even though being an empath comes with plenty of challenges and special considerations you need to make, it's possible to adjust your life to make it easier on you. With time, this will become second nature.

Chapter 3

Dealing With, Avoiding, And Cleansing Negativity

Why is being an empath so confusing? Because handing your own skills and abilities will require that you radically shift your view of the world. In addition, there is little to no understanding of empaths, and some don't even believe that they exist. A lot of empaths struggle with the wrong information and tools and thus let their abilities go to waste. But thankfully, you don't have to suffer like this.

Understanding The "Sponging" Concept

Along with this, a lot of empaths who are trained and experienced with their abilities aren't aware of how much they really do soak up other people's feelings. This is also known as "sponging" and refers to picking up on people's energies and taking them on as your own. This usually happens when there isn't enough awareness about what being an empath really means. If you think about it, perhaps it shouldn't be much of a surprise. Everyone is taught that what they feel is their own emotions. If you are happy, you are happy. When you're sad, you're just sad. But for empaths, this isn't necessarily the case. You might just be sensing other's emotions.

Knowing What Is Yours On A Deep Level

Even for those who do realize that everything they feel might not be from them, the awareness of being an empath is a complex one, and the odds are that you might still feel confused about some aspects of it. Your body of energy has multiple layers and requires a lot of sorting out. It isn't only the emotions you sense from others that matter, but also the opinions others have of high empathy that you might have internalized in the past. This can impact your self-image in a very deep way. In addition, you might have a desire that you assume is yours, when in fact you just absorbed it from someone else years ago.

Embedding Emotions Into Yourself

Perhaps what is most challenging about the skill of heightened empathy is that the energies of other people usually feel no different than your own personal emotions.

There is no flashing signal to indicate that someone else's strong emotion is heading towards you. Therefore, empaths may easily embed the energy of others into themselves without knowing what is happening. For instance, perhaps you suddenly feel sad for no real reason. You might think to yourself that you feel sad and don't know why, then instantly look for a reason to validate that emotion, such as someone at work being angry with you. This is how easy it is to embed someone else's feeling into your own energy.

Taking Responsibility

Keep in mind that you should also always take responsibility for your own feelings (yet another reason why learning how to decipher them is so important). You will need a lot of training and practice to avoid using the sponging concept as a way to avoid your own feelings. It's easy to fall into the trap of thinking "This isn't my emotion anyway, so I don't need to look at it" which is a dangerous way to think. This is just a way of blaming others for your own issues.

Keep in mind that no clear guidelines or rules exist when it comes to dealing with other people's energies versus your own. Rather, you must learn some techniques, practice them, and experiment a lot to figure out how this looks from situation to situation.

How Beliefs Impact Empath Sponging

Belief plays a large role in how sponging will impact you, as an empath. As soon as you become aware of your own beliefs that are holding you back in this area, they will instantly hold less power over you. Here are some of the most common factors that have an effect on this phenomenon.

- "All I feel is about me" - The modern western world has an assumption that if you feel something, it's about you. This can be compared to thinking of individuals as containers for their emotion, without any sharing or bleeding over happening. Therefore, the most logical assumption after this would be to believe that you should take responsibility for all your emotions.

- "My feelings are a result of my experiences" - Empaths usually engage in a lot of reflection, especially about themselves. Therefore, the assumptions that all you feel must be because of you can lead you to create reasons for your feelings. Eventually, you will have created a whole plan of action to deal with a feeling that might not have had anything to do with you, to begin with.

- "It's my job to help others" - In addition to everything, most empaths believe that they need to help other people, even when it's at their expense. It's important to realize that this trait is not inevitable and that you can change it if you wish to. However, it does contribute heavily to the challenges and struggles of being an empath. Your thoughts and beliefs work together to form your relationships with other people. Therefore, if you have a strong belief that you're responsible for helping others at your own expense, that is the reality you will experience.

As you can see, there are multiple factors that lead empaths to believe that their feelings only have to do with them. In addition, when you reflect on emotions, it's always possible to discover the reasons why they exist. So while a specific sensation or emotion might be coming from you, it's also possible that it isn't. When you just assume that all you feel is your own, you are actually opening yourself up more to this "sponging" phenomenon, helping the emotions of others stick more to you and burden you.

Fears Related To Heightened Empathy

Unfortunately, a lot of fear surrounds the idea of being highly empathetic. As soon as you begin researching the topic, you will come upon countless pages about protecting yourself from others' negativity. We will cover that a bit in this chapter, and especially in chapter five where we go over meditation and the chakra system. However, shielding should not be all you rely on. As an empath, you are going to attract the painful emotions of others because you might feel obligated to do so. However, you have more power than you may believe. Let's first look at how to shield yourself, then look beyond that.

Visualizing A Shield

Shielding can be useful for certain situations. For instance, if you have to go to a party for work where you know you are going to be surrounded by people who stress you out, knowing how to create a shield is a very valuable skill worthy of your time. To do this, just follow these simple steps:

- Go Somewhere Calm And Breathe: Do this in an area where you will not be disturbed and can get some peace and quiet. Then start to take deep breaths repeatedly for about five minutes. Once you are in a calm state, do the following.

- Envision A Bubble Of Light Around You: Imagine a glowing bubble of light surrounding your body. This can be any color you like, but most find success with white, blue, or gold.

- Believe It Will Help You: Belief is the most important aspect of any visualization exercise. You must believe with all of your heart and mind that this shield is going to protect you from any negativity that you come into contact with.

Looking Beyond Shielding

Although, as mentioned before, shielding is a valuable and helpful skill, you must also learn how to look beyond this. When you only rely on tools such as shielding, you are focusing exclusively on resistance, instead of learning how to work with your own difficulties. For some, this might create only a temporary helping effect and over the long term lead to more conflict. Here are some alternatives to techniques such as shielding.

- Observe Your Beliefs: You may find it highly helpful to pay attention to what emotions and beliefs are happening inside of you that create your experiences as an empath. When you commit to doing the work needed, you will be in control of your energy. As you make changes within yourself, you may cease fighting with external circumstances.

- Seeing The World As A Reflection: Once you start to make the changes mentioned above, the world will begin to look more like a reflection of yourself and something you can learn from. This is by no means easy, but it does pay off over time.

- How Do You Think You "Should" Act? One of the first steps you can take to protect yourself from negative influences is realizing the ways you believe you "should" act around those who make you feel bad. This is your first layer of reprogramming your beliefs.

Perhaps you will discover that you have a hard time setting up boundaries with negative influences. Shielding can help when you have no choice but to be around negative people, but it won't do much when you choose to put yourself around them due to ingrained beliefs within yourself.

- Finding The Roots: Oftentimes, beliefs about why you "should" be around people who make you feel bad have roots from years and years ago. They might have to do with how you were raised or a coping mechanism you developed in the past. Whatever the case, it's important to realize that you feel responsible for others' well-being.

Regardless of how you choose to go about it, in order to stop soaking up others' negative emotions, you will have to re-evaluate your life. What is your purpose with others? How is your current belief system working for you? Of course, trying to dismantle old mental habits is going to bring up resistance, but this is needed to become an empowered empath, rather than one who is constantly struggling and taken advantage of.

The Importance Of Nature As An Empath

For people who feel like they are struggling under the weight of other people's emotions, nature is the best way to heal. Some believe that empaths are needed to help restore the planet to a healthy balance.

- Going Outside Once A Day: The majority of negative emotions and thoughts come from human beings. So, if you have the gift of heightened empathy, you need to go out into nature by yourself every day to recharge and cleanse yourself. Walking barefoot or even sitting under a tree can do a lot to eliminate negative energies from yourself.

- Being Around Water: Water is a very healing thing to be around. Whether it's the lake, ocean, or even a pool, it's positive for empaths to make a priority in their lives. You can also connect with flowers and animals.

- Carrying Stones And Crystals: Another way you can connect with nature, as an empath, is to use stones in a protective way. It's not necessary or needed to be obsessed with protection since you are always in control of your own life situation. However, keeping focused on your energy is necessary in order to protect it from negativity.

When you stay constantly aware of your emotions and energy, you can't become a victim of other people unless you choose to do so. Your emotions and energies have to be moving constantly in order to fulfill your purpose on earth as an empath, which is to amplify, transmute, and process energy and emotion.

If you don't do this on a constant basis, you are going to be weighed down by old, stagnant energy. Carrying stones such as obsidian or clear quartz can help you keep negative energies away and can be placed in your pocket or worn on a necklace.

Other Techniques For Repelling Negativity

If you are not constantly aware of the dangers of negativity sticking to you, as an empath, you are always at risk. Being outside around water, being around animals, and carrying stones can help, but what else can you do to cleanse negativity and stay healthy and balanced?

Reading

Reading is great for empaths because it expands their perspective and helps them feel less alone. It can also provide a welcome distraction from overwhelming emotions and teach you a lot about what it means to be human. As an empath, you may be especially interested in fiction and psychology topics. You might also enjoy reading about spirituality.

Keeping A Journal

Keeping a journal is probably the best way to check in with yourself on a regular basis and decompress, in terms of thoughts and feelings. Try to write in it every day, even if it's only a paragraph. You will soon notice how much it improves your overall outlook and mood.

Making Time For Art

As mentioned before, empaths are usually very creative and artistic types of people. In order to feel okay, you must have an outlet for expressing this part of yourself. If you're going through a hard time, maybe you're also avoiding creative expression because it makes you feel things more intensely. However, creativity can be a great form of emotional healing and release to restore you to balance and cleanse negative energies.

Don't Hold Back From Crying

Empaths have a heightened emotional body, meaning that crying is necessary whenever the need arises. Crying is a healing activity and works to clear out your aura. Kids know this instinctively, which is why they cry much more than adults. As a result, they are naturally more emotionally healthy than most grown-ups.

Energy Work

Energy work such as Tai Chi or yoga can help you release stress and stay away from negativity. In addition, it can rebalance the system of chakras and realign your body.

Baths With Sea Salt

Sea salt is very helpful for cleansing negativity because it draws out energy. Try to do this on a regular basis, especially when you're feeling emotionally overwhelmed. You may use Himalayan salt, sea salt, or Epsom salt. In addition, adding essential oil to your bath can help strengthen the blend, such as eucalyptus or rosemary.

Finding The Best Technique For Your Needs

How are you to know which technique suits your needs best in terms of clearing out negative energy from your life? Starting now, you can begin experimenting with each of the techniques on this list. Use your intuition, look closely at your thoughts and reactions, and see what works best. In addition, pay close attention to what your external experiences look like, as this is a direct reflection of your inner state of mind.

Chapter 4

Controlling And Using
Your Empathetic Skill

There is a large difference between the untrained and trained empath. When you are not trained in your abilities, it means that you have the skill of being clairsentient. In other words, you have some self-care habits and inner beliefs that lead you to try to help others by absorbing their energy, often to your own disadvantage. However, an empath who is trained in their ability has the awareness and skill to become neutral in terms of the energy and emotions of others. So the trained empath will feel everything just as much but has a choice as to what to let impact them.

How Does A Trained Empath Handle Life?

For instance, an empath who is trained in their abilities will notice that they are feeling the sadness of another person, but choose to tap into this feeling to help that person get to the bottom of their sadness and find a solution. This type of help is consensually valuable and healing to both parties.

However, this action shouldn't be a daily occurrence with any person.

Therefore, an empath who is trained in their ability will also know how to notice when what they are feeling is coming from someone else and let the feeling go. This obviously requires practice and effort, but it is possible.

Blocking Balls From Your Goal

This can be compared to playing a sport and blocking balls from the goal. You will see the balls but have the ability to divert them from entering the goal. If you aren't used to playing sports, this can seem challenging or even impossible, at first. But just like anything else, awareness of energy is something that must be practiced in order to feel comfortable.

When you start reprogramming the beliefs you hold about your responsibilities to help others, and what you are responsible for taking care of, you will notice that it's easier and easier to get the balls away from the goal.

The Self-Esteem And Self-Image Of The Empath

A low self-image is a common issue for empaths, due to soaking in the energy of others, taking on responsibility for their problems, and just being confused about your own nature. To put it simply, a quality self-image means you must feel positively towards yourself and comfortable with who you are. But empaths who are not trained with their skill have taken on so many piles of emotion and energy from others that it's stuck in their body and field of energy. This can lead to physical issues and general discomfort on a mental and emotional level.

Helping Others To Feel Good

When you aren't feeling great, it's nearly impossible to feel good about yourself, and not feeling great comes along with being confused about why you feel so much. Therefore, it can be easy for empaths to judge themselves and have a low self-image.

Helping others may seem like your only method for feeling like you have a purpose. But relying too much on this will only make the issue worse. Here are some ways you can control and use your gifts for positive ends:

- Learning To Say No: Learning to set boundaries and say no to others is your first step for adequately using your skill of heightened empathy. If your energy source of empathy is being used too often, you will feel depleted and unable to help others. Thus, you should learn how to say no without guilt.

- Getting A Spiritual Teacher: The best way to master a skill is to learn from someone who has experience with it. Do some research and find a mentor either online or in person to help you wield your empathy with success.

- Reading Up On Your Gift: Knowledge is the best source of power. Therefore, you should research all you can about the phenomenon of empathy and empaths. Learning as much as you can will help you come up with a plan of action for controlling and using your skill.

- Accepting That You Aren't Responsible: Getting to deep-seated beliefs and changing them is no easy task. You may feel compelled to help others (even to your own detriment), and if this is the case, it's due to a belief you hold. You can only use your skill well when you know that you aren't obligated to help others, even if you are equipped to do so.

Going through all of the steps listed above will help you become a powerful and self-sufficient empath who is healthy and can help others when they need it. Being able to say no is the most crucial step in this and will help you form a healthy self-image.

Chapter 5

Meditation And The Chakras

Highly sensitive individuals will always respond to the external (and internal) world in a more intense way, just as empaths will always process the energy of other people in a more intense way. Sensitive wiring comes from psychological and biological reasons, while the wiring of empaths is psychological and energetic and impacts the physical body in multiple ways. When you are seeking to understand the ability of heightened empathy, you must also understand how the energetic body works.

Signs Of Untrained, Heightened Empathy

Below is a list of occurrences or situations that may seem familiar or show you that you are an unidentified or untrained empath. Keep in mind that experienced and trained empaths probably will not relate to the points listed, but then this book may not be necessary for them to begin with.

If you're already experienced with your empath skills, try to remember what signals gave away your nature. Keep in mind that when you find out you're an empath, you might think that a lot of others around you are too, but that is not necessarily the case. Here are the signs that you may be an untrained empath:

- People Are Comfortable Sharing With You: If you are an untrained empath, you have probably been told by others that they feel a lot better once they share their emotional or even physical problems with you, but you sometimes feel worse once a situation like this occurs. In addition, some individuals may feel uncomfortable with you because they think you can always tell what they are thinking or feeling.

- Sudden, Unexplained Emotions: You have felt pains and aches, or very intense feelings seemingly out of the blue, then discovered later on that a person close to you also experienced it around the same time.

- Crowds Are Intense For You: Any time you are in a crowded room, the physical sensations and emotions you experience get very intense and also shift quickly from minute to minute, leading you to think you might be crazy. However, when you leave the crowd, these feelings instantly dissipate.

- Trouble With Concentration: You have a difficult time focusing when you are around others, but this problem disappears any time you are alone.

- Intuitive Knowing About Others: You have always been able to sense a lot about people, even though you don't know where the information comes from. This may seem normal to you because you're so used to it.

- A Sense Of Obligation: As an untrained empath, you are probably familiar with feeling obligated to care for and help those in your life. You might also be told often that you should calm down or stop worrying so much, but it's hard for you.

- Changing Moods: Any time you get around specific people, you may notice that you suddenly think, feel, or act differently. But when you aren't around them anymore, you are back to normal.

- Confusion About Your Needs: You might have a hard time knowing exactly what you need and want out of life. In order to figure this out, alone time is required. However, even when you do think you've figured it out, you find yourself stating what others expect from you rather than your true needs.

- A Hard Time Setting Boundaries: Setting boundaries and saying no to others often results in anger and disappointment from others that is hard for you to handle. It may seem as though regardless of what you do, you can't find a good solution and have to choose between letting others down or bending to their will and getting overwhelmed.

- You Crave Distraction: You often feel unpleasant and dark physically for no discernible reason, which makes you want to seek out distractions to take this feeling away. For this reason, drugs and alcohol may appeal to you more than the average person, and you might even struggle with addictions.

- Eye Contact Is Intense For You: You may feel another person's emotions or energy more strongly when you are making direct eye contact with them. For this reason, you often look away to avoid discomfort in these situations.

Keep in mind that the points above are supposed to help you identify whether you are an untrained empath, and in order to be one, you don't have to recognize each of the signs. This is just meant to shed some light on who you are. If you found yourself agreeing with a lot of them, you should accept that being an empath is a high possibility for you, but make sure you reflect on this more if you still aren't sure. Also, keep in mind that the points above don't define what it means to be an empath. Therefore, if you've talked to people who think that empaths have it really bad, the odds are that they are just an untrained empath who doesn't know how to handle their own ability.

Suffering Is Not Necessary

There is a belief out there that being an empath means endless suffering, but this is not true. However, you have to teach yourself how to handle your skill. This will require time and effort but will transform your life in amazing ways. As soon as you decide to commit to becoming an empowered empath, you will learn how to navigate crowds with ease and handle difficult situations in a whole new way. This is because your internal view would have shifted.

If you usually discuss situations in terms of feelings, vibes, and energy, you might be an empath. You might have noticed that you feel high empathy in situations that others don't, or that your emotions seem exceptionally intense when you're tired.

Clearing And Cleansing Yourself

Daily associations and emotional interactions might leave you feeling very sensitive or in need of a way to shake off the emotions you've soaked up. For the empath, physically and empathetic in-tune activities are necessary for staying sane. This involves chakra clearing and a reliable, consistent practice of meditation. In this section, we will cover some ideas for staying spiritually balanced, even throughout the overwhelming energetic exchanges and bombardments of your daily life. We will also cover the system of the chakras. Performing meditation while focusing on certain chakras will help you release blockages that can result in emotional, physical, or spiritual issues and imbalances.

The Levels Of Your Energetic Field (The Chakras)

The energy field of human beings radiates externally, like an aura that surrounds your entire body. The human field of energy contains seven levels that begin physically and extend outward. Here they are:

1. The red etheric body or root chakra.

2. The orange emotional body or sacral chakra.

3. The yellow mental body or solar plexus.

4. The green heart chakra or higher mental field.

5. The turquoise spirit body or throat chakra.

6. The casual dark blue body or third eye.

7. The violet higher self or crown chakra.

You can learn to expand your understanding by first understanding the chakra system, then eventually gain a higher awareness of how energetic levels line up to the colors and chakras from your body. In order to get a whole chakra meditation, you may begin with working through each of the following meditations at one time, or just focusing on one on its own.

The Root Chakra

The red root chakra is the primary chakra of the seven systems. In this chakra, you are controlled by your survival needs and tribal instinct, including the ego, sexuality, and family. It's necessary to clean out this energy system and discover support and grounding at your root before you proceed to the higher levels. If you notice that you are cut off from this chakra, you can use breath work to switch yourself into a new frame of consciousness.

- Sit Up Straight: Begin by sitting down in a position that is comfortable for you, with your back straight and your spine stretched out. You can sit in a chair with your feet touching the ground or cross-legged on a cushion or the ground.

- Visualize: Next, you should envision red in your mind, imagining that the color is becoming more distinct, brighter, and clearer. Start breathing in deeply, then exhale, as you imagine your root becoming melded to the ground, giving you strength and stability.

- Focus On Your Physical Body: Become extremely aware of your breathing as you sense the energy of your life force spinning and buzzing inside of you and especially in your lower body. While you focus on red, imagine your energy root uncoiling and moving upward through your whole body, along with your spine and up to your head. Try to run through the steps listed above repeatedly and do this for at least 10 minutes. Being outside helps a lot with this particular meditation.

Your Sacral Chakra

The next chakra on the list is the sacral chakra. Moving your focus up to your spine, think about the color orange, which represents creativity, addictions, and relationships with others. Engaging in creativity is a great way to activate this chakra's energy. Here are some examples of activities that will help with that:

- Painting or drawing.

- Yoga, or Tai chi.

- Dancing and singing.

It's also possible to shift directly from the root chakra exercise above into your sacral chakra, which exists just below your belly button. Just imagine orange energy brightly spinning and clearing out any blockages within this chakra system. Try to breathe in at least 10 times until it feels clear. When you begin to feel lighter, it's time to move onto the next chakra.

The Yellow Solar Plexus

The solar plexus chakra is signified by the color yellow and has to do with your friendships, fears, personal power, and social life. As an empath, you are sensitive and often drained by being around other people, so this chakra is taking most of the load. You should be mindful enough to clear this out on a regular basis. Here's how to deal with that:

- Recognize The Stress: Whenever you feel changes or stress, you might notice that you feel butterflies, digestive issues, or other issues with your tummy. You can handle this by meditating on the color yellow, then doing the following visual exercises.

- Imagine Yourself Poised And Ready: As you think about the color yellow, run through visualizations of yourself going through daily life with a calm and composed attitude. Keep in mind that you are protected from harmful negativity outside of you.

- Breathe: As you go through the steps listed above, make sure you are breathing thoroughly and deeply. Do this anytime you are feeling nervous or unsure of yourself.

The Green Heart Chakra

It's possible to attract a healthy and loving partner, but first, your heart chakra has to be opened and cleansed before you will be ready. Since this is about your heart, it may be obvious that things can be stored here. As you might have guessed, this is where you store energy from childhood issues, rejection, compassion, and love. Here is how to keep this chakra balanced and healthy:

- Think Of A Green Rose: First, imagine green energy forming a rose shape in the middle of the chest while you breathe in and out. As you inhale and exhale, imagine that the rose is opening wider and wider.

- Letting Go Of Negativity: As the flower's petals unfold slowly, allow your heart to feel open as you clear out any negative emotion or energy that was stuck within the flower. If you don't see it growing at first, be patient. If this visualization is a challenge, accept that you might have some unresolved emotions and keep working on it until it goes well.

Your Throat Chakra

The sensation of a lump in your throat may be familiar to you. Everyone has said or felt this themselves when they have wanted to say something but couldn't find the words or held back tears in an emotional moment. This is because their throat chakra was engaged and blocked. This is the center responsible for self-expression and communication with the outside world. Whenever you have a hard time finding the right words for your thoughts, this chakra likely needs to be cleansed. Here is how to do that:

- Imagine Turquoise: Imagine a bright turquoise color where your throat is, then inhale and exhale with your mouth open. Each time you breathe in, take the pure light inward, then imagine it flowing out each time you release the breath.

- Embody Truth: As you do this, try to feel the truth, liberation, and sincerity with each and every breath, allowing true expression of the self to fill you up.

- Be Mindful Of Your Self-Talk: As you engage in this exercise, make sure that your inner voice is only speaking in gentle and truthful terms. This will help your self-confidence soar and bloom fully.

Your Third Eye

The next chakra is the third eye, which exists right in the middle of your eyebrows. This part of you handles your higher knowing and intuition throughout life. The true goal of aligning each of your chakras is to be able to live from this chakra center every day. In order to connect with your inner knowledge and imagination, just close your eyes and meditate on this part of your body, then imagine your brain lighting up with energy until your mind clears.

Your Crown Chakra

As you work through each of the previous six chakras, you will finally come to your crown chakra, which exists above and outside of you and is connected to something higher. This helps you stay connected to higher forces instead of getting stuck in lower fields of energy that can be exhausting. To unblock this field of energy, simply imagine a Lotus at the top of your head as you breathe life into your body and up your spine. Working on each of these chakras on a regular basis will help you immensely.

Chapter 6

Tips For Thriving
As An Empath

This book has already given you some useful tools for thriving as an empath. Your gift does not have to feel like a curse. Here are some methods for making the most of who you are and helping others while staying healthy and balanced.

Tips For Thriving With Your Skill

These days, we are always bombarded with negativity, making it challenging to thrive with your sensitive personality. Even if you stay at home in your safe space, you will still absorb feelings from outside of you, leading you to seek distraction or feel drained. In order to fight this fate, you have to know how to stay grounded and protect yourself.

All people are different and require different techniques for this, but the most important aspect is staying healthy physically while quieting your mind. Here are some ways to achieve that:

Getting Plenty Of Water:

Our bodies are 75 percent water, so it plays a large role in healing oneself. Most people don't get enough water and hardly even realize that they are dehydrated.

- Eight Cups Per Day: Not getting enough water will give you issues both physically and energetically, while speeding up the process of aging and harming your general health. You should drink a minimum of eight cups of water each day in order to replenish yourself. The more you weigh, the more you should drink.

- A Nice Shower: Water clears away dirt and negativity, making your energy body clean again. If you don't believe this, next time you have a hard day, rather than reaching for some alcohol, take a shower instead. You will notice that this immediately clears your mind and mood.

Paying Attention To Your Diet:

An essential lifestyle change for the empath is paying more attention to your diet. Nutritious meals can change your entire life if you decide to prioritize this. Stay away from anything processed, soda, and sugar.

- It's Not About What Others Do: Changing the diet can be a huge challenge because it's "normal" to eat horrible foods every day. But although many others eat this way, you are sensitive and probably react more strongly to it.

- Avoid Low Vibration Foods: Everything vibrates at differing frequencies, and this includes alcohol, drugs, and foods. The higher something vibrates, the better it is. When it comes to low vibrations, empaths are impacted in a serious way. If you have a hard time staying grounded or balanced, check your diet first.

- Examples Of What To Eat: Healthy foods to prioritize in your life include plenty of fresh fruits and vegetables, nuts and seeds, fish and chicken, and natural fat sources such as coconut oil or pure butter. Stay away from candy, enriched flour, and fried foods as these will harm you.

Energy Balancing

We've talked a bit about the importance of balancing energies. Now, this is important for everyone out there, but it's absolutely essential to survival for the empath. When you make sure to balance your feminine and masculine energies, you will be more emotionally stable and strong throughout life. Meditate on what it means to you to be masculine and feminine and make sure you have a healthy attitude towards both energies. When you pursue health and meditate on a regular basis, these energies will naturally align to what they are meant to be.

Staying Active Every Day

Just as nutrition is essential for mental and emotional balance, as an empath, exercise is also extremely important. A lot of people in the modern world think about exercise only in terms of becoming more toned and losing weight. But that's only a tiny portion of the big picture. Exercise can be very beneficial for many more reasons, particularly for sensitive empaths. Here is what it can do for you:

- Release Tension: Exercise is the perfect way to get rid of pent-up feelings and get rid of emotional impurities. This is true not only emotionally, but physically as it cleans out toxins in the body while also enhancing your state of mind.

- Gives You More Energy: Being an empath can be exhausting, so you need all the energy you can get. Instead of reaching for the coffee, try doing some intense exercise instead. This will offer you a burst of energy that lasts throughout the day instead of giving you a crash.

- Grounds You: Earlier, we talked about how important it is to have a strong root chakra (the chakra system responsible for your physical well-being). Exercising can help you feel more grounded in your physical body while also making you stronger.

- Strengthens You: Everyone knows that exercise makes you stronger but did you know that a stronger body protects you more against bad energies and negative emotions from outside of you? This is yet another reason to make exercise a regular part of your life. You can start with taking short walks each day and working your way up to longer bouts of exercise. Jump, stretch, and dance to get your pulse up and you will soon feel much better!

Balancing The Chakras Regularly

Everyone has seven main chakra centers that run throughout their bodies. These systems are the seats of your power on a spiritual level and correspond with your hormones and organs. When any of the seven is blocked or unbalanced, it will lead to physical and mental issues. Make sure you follow the steps outlined in the previous chapter in order to keep these systems in order and functioning the way they should. You will notice a difference quite quickly if you stick to this.

Regular Meditation:

Meditation is absolutely essential for getting a hold of your fearful thoughts and endless mind noise. Having a chaotic, busy mind can be very stressful and keeps you ungrounded. Meditation will bring you useful insights and help you handle stress with ease. You can start with the chakra meditations listed in the previous chapter, but feel free to explore outside of this, here are some examples of delving deeper into meditation:

- Doing Walking Meditations: Sitting still and quieting your mind can be a challenge at first, so walking meditations helps a lot especially when you are a beginner. To do this, simply walk outside in nature in a quiet area and focus entirely on each step you take, while breathing deeply. Anytime your mind wanders, don't worry, simply return to focusing on your steps and breathing. With time, this will become much easier and more calming, then you can move onto the steps below.

- Guided Meditations: Many people benefit by looking up guided meditations online and listening to them. This is helpful to start with, especially for beginners, because it gives you something to listen to and focus on. Eventually, you can do it without audio.

- Joining a Group: Meditation groups can be a great initiation to meditation since you have someone walking you through it. In addition, being surrounded by others with the same goal as you (quieting your mind) can do wonders for your focus. Look online to see if there are any active meditation groups in your area or look to join one online.

Making Time For Humor

Being an empath can feel heavy and dark, at times, which is why humor is such a useful tool. Children naturally laugh and have fun all the time, but adults often forget how to do this because they take life so seriously. Make time in your schedule for funny movies and make sure you are spending plenty of quality time with those who make you laugh. This will keep you in balance throughout all of the challenges of daily life.

Escaping Pollution

We talked a bit about the importance of spending time in nature, earlier in the book. Being in a polluted environment isn't just harmful to your body, but also harms you mentally and emotionally. Make sure that you are making time for green surroundings at least once a day. In addition, clearing pollution out is more than just an environmental concern and also involves staying clean mentally. Take note of your negative thought habits and make sure you are keeping them in check.

Keeping Good Influences Around

Your environment has a huge impact on who you are, whether you realize it or not. Do you have friends in your life that end up causing you more harm than good? It's time to do yourself a favor and spend less time with them. Instead, seek out positive influences to keep around you, and your life will change.

Using Aromatherapy

Scent has a large impact on your state of mind. Aromatherapy, including essential oils and scented candles, can be a great tool for you to add to your life. Essential oils have been used for many years and can help you with relaxation, re-balancing, grounding, protection, energy, and more. Cinnamon, for example, can invigorate you and protect you against nausea, while lavender can calm you down and soothe you to sleep. You can take baths with these oils or even use them as perfume. Do some research to find out which scent suits you best.

Remember That Changes Take Practice

As you can see, there are plenty of useful, easy, and free techniques for staying healthy and balanced as an empath. However, these changes will take lots of practice. Keep in mind that the way you live now did not magically appear overnight but has happened due to a long string of choices. Therefore, you can begin to make new choices and change the course of your life at any time. You can be an empowered individual who is not ashamed of your gifts, as an empath but is instead proud to be who you are. Is this possible for you?

This level of self-esteem is not only possible but the natural result of working at it over time. With this information, you are ready to thrive and be the best you possible! Good luck on your journey.

Conclusion

Thank you for reading "Empath: How To Protect Yourself From Negativity And Thrive As An Empath". It's my hope that you now see this personality trait as an asset and not as a hindrance.

You need to know your purpose as an empath, or you will always struggle. This starts with setting boundaries and prioritizing your own peace of mind. Although this will feel difficult and foreign, if you aren't used to it, it's more than possible to do once you commit to the path.

Empaths have a unique ability to heal the world. However, it's important that you also know how to care for yourself in the process, so you don't get taken advantage of by negative influences or get overwhelmed. Feel free to read this book over and over and refer back to the tools listed within it anytime you need some extra guidance.

30409850R00188

Printed in Great Britain
by Amazon